The Accidental Lutheran

The Accidental Lutheran

The Journey
from Heidelberg to Wittenberg

Nancy A. Almodovar

Foreword by Craig Kellerman

RESOURCE *Publications* • Eugene, Oregon

THE ACCIDENTAL LUTHERAN
The Journey from Heidelberg to Wittenberg

Resource Publications
An Imprint of Wipf and Stock Publishers
199 W. 8th Ave., Suite 3
Eugene, OR 97401

www.wipfandstock.com

PAPERBACK ISBN: 978-1-5326-6816-6
HARDCOVER ISBN: 978-1-5326-6817-3
EBOOK ISBN: 978-1-5326-6818-0

Manufactured in the U.S.A. June 13, 2019

Dedication

This book is first dedicated to my husband, Bobby. We made this journey out of modern evangelicalism back to the "first evangelicals" (aka Lutheranism) together. I could not imagine anyone else I would want to take this journey with in this life. May the Lord Jesus Christ, who first brought us together, continue to teach us the True Faith as we travel in this sinful, sad, and fallen world to our heavenly home with our great and gracious Triune God.

Second, I must thank my new church family at Faith Lutheran. You welcomed us with open arms, teaching us the unadulterated Word of God and living it before us. I especially want to thank the Ladies Tuesday Bible Study and the Dorcas Women's Group as your encouragement, patience, sacrificial giving, and love for Christ and others exemplify the character of true women of God. Very special thanks to both Debby and Janet who worked to proofread and edit the manuscript so that this book could come to completion.

Thank you for your love and friendship.—"*I just remembered my baptism*."

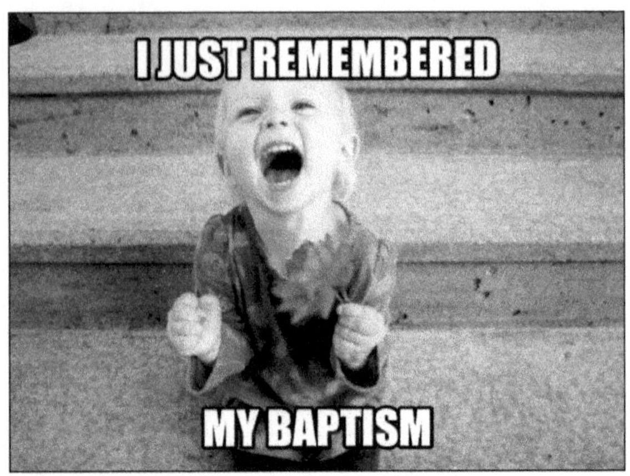

Finally, this book is dedicated to those who know there is something more in the Lord's Supper and baptism than what they have been taught in either evangelical or Reformed churches. This is for my friends who wanted to know why we left the Reformed/ Calvinist view of Scripture and converted to Lutheranism. It is my constant prayer that Christ will shine His light on His Word in a way that teaches us what He has plainly said is what He meant. For those struggling with assurance may you find that in His baptismal waters there is a true peace and quietness and in, with and under the bread and wine He feeds us His true body and blood to strengthen our weak faith.

If you have found this book and do not yet know Christ, I pray you will read the gospel in every page and be brought from darkness to light so that you too

"*. . . may receive the forgiveness of sins and an inheritance among those who are sanctified by faith in Christ.*"

ACTS 26:18

Contents

Foreword by Craig Kellerman | ix

Introduction | xiii

CHAPTER 1 A Wintry Hindrance by a Providential Hand | 1

CHAPTER 2 Lutheran Undercurrents | 9

CHAPTER 3 Something More—Hoc Est Corpus Meum | 13

CHAPTER 4 God's Own Child—The Forgiveness of Sins through the Waters of Baptism | 42

CHAPTER 5 Comfort—Simple and True | 85

Bibliography | 93

Foreword

Rev. Craig Kellerman,
Faith Lutheran Church (LCMS),
Mountain Home, ID

Though the author describes herself as the "*Accidental Lutheran,*" it pleases me to say that she has become "*The Intentional Lutheran,*" as this book clearly points out.

The connection with Bobby and Nancy Almodovar has truly been a Godsend to both me and our entire congregation. When Bobby and Nancy first visited our congregation, I did not get an opportunity to have a lengthy conversation with them other than the usual greeting in the narthex. Then I noticed that they signed the guest book as Rev. Bobby and Dr. Nancy Almodovar. Bobby was ordained in the Assemblies of God International Fellowship church and Nancy had her doctorate in apologetics. She also had been ordained. It was a few weeks later, that they visited our church once more. This time I learned that they were members of the Dutch Reformed Church (URC-NA) in Boise, Idaho and were visiting here because of the bad winter weather. I mistakenly thought that this would probably be the last of it as they seemed committed to that congregation.

After some time passed, I received notice from "Worship for Shut-ins" (now "Worship Anew") that Nancy and Bobby had been listening to the broadcast and wanted someone from the Lutheran

Church to contact them. Shamefully I did not respond right away as I had some apprehension as to what I might be getting myself into. When I did contact Nancy, she informed me that they were looking for a Reformed church here in town so that they would not have to travel so far. She wanted to be able to attend mid-week Bible studies and activities. More flags went up! The LCMS does not fit the billing as to what most people consider to be "Reformed." I didn't need to have someone challenging what I was teaching or leading the members astray. Boy, was I wrong! God knew what He was doing.

By the end of the conversation, I invited her to come to the Ladies Bible Study that meets on Tuesday afternoon and assured her that the group would welcome her with open arms. She came to the Bible study and the next Sunday they were in church.

The rest is, as they say, history. We immediately scheduled some visits in which I was able to thoroughly discuss with them the differences between Lutheran theology and modern day Reformed theology. As Nancy is quite a scholar, I gave her some of my books to read and a list of other materials. She couldn't get enough and discussed it with Bobby. They were led by the Holy Spirit to accept Lutheran doctrine as being the true interpretation of Scripture and were confirmed into membership.

Nancy and Bobby have proven to be a great asset to our congregation and to me as they bring with them a great deal of insight into what the "reformed" churches teach and confess.

In this book, *The Accidental Lutheran*, Nancy addresses two of the important doctrines of the Christian faith, specifically the sacraments of baptism and the Lord's Supper, which along with the Word we refer to as the "Means of Grace." Having been part of Pentecostal and then "reformed" churches almost all of her life, she has first-hand experience and knowledge.

This book will be of significant value to those people who are looking for answers to the questions that might be nagging at their hearts. It is also a good resource to those people who have been life-long Lutherans. It is a good refresher course and it will help them understand where Christians from other denominational persuasions are coming from.

And so it is that I thank God for Nancy's devotion to the Word and her zeal for sharing these "newfound" truths with anyone and everyone who might listen.

Introduction

The journey to Lutheranism seemed to begin out of necessity in 2017. However, it was long before the day that we walked into Faith Lutheran (LCMS) here in Mountain Home, Idaho, that God had already been *Lutheran-izing* us. This is the story of how we became the Accidental Lutheran and traveled the theological roads from Heidelberg (Calvinism/Reformed) and ended up in Wittenberg (as Gene Edward Veith Jr. calls them "the first evangelicals[1]" and Lutheran).

In July 2013 I completed my doctorate degree in theology, having worked on the proverbial "Problem of Evil." This is where my own inner longings began to swirl around in my mind and heart as I searched the "secret things which belong to God alone." What I had anticipated as being the solution to the philosophical and often theological issues of evil, death, sickness, and problems, ended up rocking my own assurance of salvation and a longing burst open in my own heart for a God who was merciful, loving, and kind. While His justice was understood and believed, i.e., we are sinners in rebellion against our Creator and God, if I pressed the teaching in the Reformed world regarding the elective purposes of God and His providence, it left me wondering whether or not I was even among the elect myself. Panic attacks would awaken me in the early hours of morning as to whether or not I was saved, redeemed, and more specifically, whether I was one of God's elect or just one of His reprobates. I would lay there wondering if I had

1. Veith, *Spirituality of the Cross*, 15.

simply fooled myself and others that I was a believer. In the end, I would wonder, whether I would find that I really was not among those for whom Christ Jesus had died for. When I looked within my own heart the realization was this: Here lies the true problem of evil: my sins stared back angrily accusing me while Satan's darts of doubt found their place in poisoning any assurance I had. Panic led to spiritual depression and questions about my eternal state.

The admonitions from pastors and friends alike were to look within to see if you love the Law, if you are following God's commands, and if you are producing fruit worthy of repentance. Were you trusting in the work of Christ or not? Did you truly repent and believe or not? However, this did not solve my struggle but only exacerbated it a hundredfold. Being in a position of influence amongst women coming out of more Arminian and evangelical churches left me feeling I was fooling both myself and them. When they doubted, I would tell them to look to Christ. Yet, in my own struggles the advice from ministers to me was to look within. Those who came out of Arminian churches were taught to focus within. They were to gain their assurance from following rules and regulations such as "Did you have your morning devotions today?" "Are you producing the fruits of the spirit?" "Am I doing enough to prove I'm a true believer?" "Are all three parts of true faith evidenced in my life?" So my advice to them was to look to Jesus alone while the advice to me, and also from others, was to look within. The women I worked with—who were coming out of works-based churches and were what Luther would call enthusiasts—were asking the same questions I was. How can I be sure I was saved? Did I have true faith? Was I deluded into thinking I was going to heaven? Under this Calvinist system I was crushed.

I often wondered why I had not taken my own advice to others. The reason? How could I know I was among the elect of God when all I saw was wretched within? If Christ only died for some, how could I know I was among that small group and not fooling myself into thinking I was? Yet here in Scripture I found that Christ is the propitiation for the world, that God so loved the world, that Jesus died for sinners of which I am definitely one. Struggling with assurance, the Reformed (Calvinistic) view held out no true hope because their source of assurance was within the sinner; i.e., look to your fruit, etc. Instead, in Lutheranism I found the Scriptures plainly read and knowing I am a sinner and in this world I would come to find that Jesus' death covered me completely, simply because I am a sinner in this world and Jesus died for the world full of sinners.

The Reformed (Calvinist) answer would be to look at your fruit to make sure that you had true faith and, for some, that they had true repentance. Teaching them, I would often remind these ladies of what the Heidelberg Catechism says about true faith and then admonish them to look within for assurance. After all, this is what I was doing, what I was taught to do. I had to look within for proof I was saved and this created a problem for me. It was at that point that I began to sense I had to look outside my experience, my feelings, and my knowledge, and I took a line from one of the Luther movies when he was struggling. In the scene Luther is frightened and unsure about his work and his salvation. His confessor tells him, "Look to Christ. Look to Christ and His work . . . " This was like a shot in the arm and I began to slowly heed that advice. The contradiction remained, however, between what I encouraged others to do and what I did with my own struggles of assurance. Yes, even knowing that God leads us, sometimes we are a little slow to follow. But what would happen several years later gave me true hope, true assurance, and an understanding that I am truly forgiven.

One key hymn which kept popping up as I worked on God's Providence in my dissertation was that written by William Cowper. He certainly understood that one must cling to Christ in the midst of the storm as he battled depression. Here the lyrics remind believers that God is certainly in control, yet we should not peer into the secret things of God too deeply as they belong to Him alone.

> God moves in a mysterious way
> His wonders to perform;
> He plants His footsteps in the sea

And rides upon the storm.

Ye fearful saints, fresh courage take;
The clouds ye so much dread
Are big with mercy and shall break
In blessings on your head.[2]

This little book is about how God providentially led my husband and me out of the Reformed theological understanding of His Word to become Confessional Lutherans (LCMS). This work focuses mostly on the longing in my heart to have a church closer to home but in God's mysterious way He led us into, as a friend calls it, the Church of the Augsburg Confession (aka Lutheranism).

Many of my Presbyterian and Reformed friends have wondered what happened, why we changed, and what Lutherans really believe. Well, I can answer the first two clearly but if you want to know more of what Lutherans believe I highly recommend reading the Book of Concord. It was there that I found I no longer had to answer every question nor did I have to have all the answers to what God has clearly and plainly not answered in His Word. It was also here in Lutheranism that I found I no longer had to do mental, philosophical, or theological gymnastics but could take God's Word plainly and simply and leave the rest to Him who knows all things. It is my intention to write with collegiality and love, understanding that some who read this may still hold fast to the Three Forms of Unity (Belgic Confession, Heidelberg Catechism and Canons of Dordt, the Dutch Reformed Confessions), the Westminster Confessions, and the Calvinistic acronym TULIP (Total Depravity, Undeserved Favor, Limited Atonement, Irresistible Grace, and Preservation of the Saints). However, they may be struggling with these issues and perhaps keep seeing Scripture teach something other than what they have learned in the Reformed, Presbyterian, Reformed Baptist, or Calvinist theological streams. This book is for you. I have undertaken this task not only

2. William Cowper, "God Moves in a Mysterious Way" (1774).

so that you understand why someone from the theological world of Heidelberg would move over to Wittenberg embracing, believing, and confessing Lutheranism but that you too might find a roadmap to the Church of the Augsburg Confession.

Throughout this book I will be comparing directly from the Heidelberg Catechism and Belgic Confession, which contain what the Dutch Reformed believe of these doctrines, with that of Concordia (the Book of Concord), which are the Lutheran Confessions. This is in order that the reader may be able to compare and contrast their views while viewing what the Scriptures say. It is my goal that the Scriptures will lead and guide you on your own theological journey.

Chapter 1

A Wintry Hindrance by a Providential Hand

It began on Thanksgiving evening in 2016 and did not end until the end of April 2017. Snow . . . snow . . . and more snow. Bobby and I had moved here to Idaho in 2014 and our dear friends would tell us, when we asked about the winters here, "Oh, no problem. We might get two or even four inches but by noon it is all melted away." Ha! While winter 2015 did go that way, the winter of 2016 was not going to let up . . . at all it seemed. Eventually, winter 2017 became known as "Snowmageddon" here in Idaho. Every weekend there were snow storms. Not two or four inches but ten, sixteen, and twenty inches at a clip. Over and over we were blocked in. It was different here than living in the big city. Back in New York City the plows would be out the moment an inch or two fell. Not here in small town, USA. The one neighbor in our cul-de-sac who had a mini-plow had moved back east so we were literally stuck in ice and snow. Knowing that God is very much in charge of the weather, we realized His providential hand in the difficulties we experienced that winter were His way of leading us out of Calvinism and Reformed teaching to a local Lutheran church and eventually to embracing Lutheran theology as the true understanding of the Scriptures.

Up to this point we had been attending a Dutch Reformed church in Boise, some 50 miles away. We loved this little church. It was growing and they loved to talk about God's word and theology even outside of service. The church we had come from back east highly recommended it to us. However, getting there in the winter months was proving impossible as the roads grew more and more impassable and treacherous. On top of snow we would have quick thaws and then blisteringly cold temperatures that would leave sheets of ice all along the route out of our development. We tried to stay in contact with our new friends at the Reformed church but the distance was proving that to be easier said than done. Emails, social media, and phone calls were becoming our only connection and those were quickly fading as the harsh winter marched onward with record snowfalls and thick, dangerous ice-covered roads.

By January we had not been to church since Thanksgiving and I was longing for the preached Word and fellowship with other believers. This was not going to happen with the weather impeding us and both Bobby and I were beginning to feel the separation. Then, one Sunday morning, frustrated that we were snowed in again, we looked at the religious channels. We hadn't done that since we left the evangelical church. However, we figured we might find something a bit more biblical than the Charismatics and, as God providentially directed, we did. This program was called Worship for Shut-Ins and now titled Worship Anew.[1] It was run by the Lutheran Church Missouri Synod and was solid; it balanced sermons of law and gospel with both new and familiar hymns interspersed.

We sat, watched, listened, and even sang along with the old hymns. It was Lutheran. It was liturgical. The pastor even wore a white robe. Well, we knew that some Lutherans were solid Christians and faithful to God's word, so we watched and were fed. Afterwards, I looked up the website, connected with it via email and we felt a bit refreshed. At least we can get the preached Word until spring . . . or so we thought.

1. "Worship Anew," LCMS Production Worship Anew. https://worshipanew.org/.

Each Sunday, with every weekend snowstorm, we would sit ourselves down and together watch Worship for Shut-Ins. I would even sing along with some of the choir pieces and solos that were part of the program when I knew the old hymns. Some of these hymns, though, we'd never heard. However, they were rich and deep and I soon came to learn the *Lutheran Service Book* is filled with hymns that speak of Christ and His work, salvation by grace and faith alone, the Lord's Supper . . . and baptism as God's work alone. We were being fed on good, solid, biblical food. Then came the longing to share this with other believers each week, but this just didn't happen.

Saturdays we would prepare to go to church in Boise and then . . . snow and ice . . . ice and more snow. Now, because my dissertation was on God's Providence, I was beginning to "get it." God was hindering us from heading up to Boise. The connections on social media were dropping as we missed service after service. The phone calls began to wane and emails were less and less frequent. Separation from our church family, no longer just by 50 miles, but by communication, was beginning to take its toll. Hungry for more than just a 30-minute program, though that was helping, we longed to join with the body of Christ to worship and praise our Savior and our God and partake of the Lord's Supper.

Bobby and I would talk . . . well, mostly I would tell him the longing of my heart. I missed being with God's people and if winters were always going to be like this one, then we needed to begin attending somewhere in town. Back east we had attended church 40+ miles from home and often I felt the lack of being with other believers as well. However, I was so busy on finishing up my doctorate, then helping Bobby as he went through radiation for prostate cancer, that I did not feel the disconnect as strongly as I was here in Idaho. Many times during the week I would ask, "Could we just visit the Lutheran church here in town?" Bobby's answer would change the course of our lives: "Sure, go check them out and we can visit."

I wasn't sure Bobby was ready to change churches just because I needed something closer to home but he heard my plea and I contacted Worship for Shut-Ins to see what church in town (there were two Lutheran ones we knew of) would be good for us to attend. A few days later an email came that Faith Lutheran was a member of the Lutheran Church Missouri Synod, which we knew to be more faithful to God's word than the other Lutheran denomination. I contacted Faith Lutheran and determined that the next Sunday we would visit.

Well, that Sunday came and Bobby was under the weather so I got ready to go to church alone. I walked in, took a seat in a pew near the middle, and sat waiting for the service to begin. I looked around at the stained glass and the beautiful pulpit and altar in the front, and began to flip through the hymnal (which is actually a service book with the whole liturgy in it). Pastor Kellerman approached me and asked if I was Nancy. I said yes and told him that Bobby was ill so I was there alone that day. He welcomed me and a few minutes later service began.

Though I was familiar with most of the order of service, it was a shock when the pastor gave absolution to everyone there. We had corporately confessed our sins as well as had a moment to privately confess them and then the pastor said that he stood in the place of Christ and forgave us. I was shocked to say the least, because who was this man to forgive our sins? I must have missed this at the Lutheran church we had visited in Brooklyn, which friends of ours attend, because this just stunned me. It wasn't so much that a man was standing there forgiving me as I read in the service book the words he just said, it was the sense of hearing in my own ears that Christ had forgiven me all my sins that was a bit shocking. In the Dutch Reformed churches you are given *assurance* your sins are forgiven, if you have repented and believed, but here I was being told "Your sins are forgiven you . . ." Writing this just doesn't bring out the impact of that truth but it awakened me within to the reality of hearing from Christ, "daughter, your sins are forgiven . . ."

As the service continued it seemed to focus completely on the work and words of Christ. Now, the Reformed also focus on Christ but there is always this sense that you have to check yourself to make sure you are in the faith. While that practice is biblical, the difference is that the Reformed concept of where that proof is found is exactly where the waters get muddied. In the Dutch Reformed church you look at the fruit you've produced to make sure you are a Christian and that you have true faith. However, in this service, I was hearing that we are to look at God's work in our baptism and that this faith is fed and nourished on the true blood and true body of our Lord Jesus in the sacrament of the altar, the Lord's Supper. In the sermon, the pastor reminded us that even as believers we can never follow God's law perfectly because we are still sinners. However, Christ did it for us and then gives us Himself in the body and blood of the Lord's Supper to sustain us. The focus was on this work of Christ which is completely, totally, 100 percent outside of us. Faith is given by God through the sacraments and then sustained in us through the Word and sacrament.

As a Reformed gal, the sacraments were not that powerful. They were "signs and seals" of God's work but they did not actually confer God's work to the recipient. This service opened my ears to hear God's call of absolution and then how He serves us in the Sunday worship service. As I left, though the Lord's Supper was not given that Sunday, I was full. Then a young man, Dennis, came over, asked my name, and if I were married. I said I was and that my husband was home sick. His immediate response was, "Oh, we will pray for him. Hope to see you again next week." That greatly impressed me almost as much as the service itself; though I have to be honest, I was not used to following along with the liturgy through the service book. Still I went home filled with the preached word of God. As I shared with Bobby how the service was, the topic of the sermon, and how friendly everyone was, he said we could go again next Sunday.

A few weeks later in early May, we received a phone call from our pastor in Boise. We had not heard from him for five months and at that point and I was not feeling very missed. During the call I shared how we were visiting the Lutheran church in town as the winter had kept us away. I will never forget his words: "Well, if you have to attend an imperfect church I suppose you have to . . ." That struck me in two ways. First, throughout our becoming Reformed we were always told that Lutherans are our brothers and sisters in the faith, only that Luther didn't go as far as he should in reforming the church and Calvin finished Luther's work of reformation. Second was a question I had to think about: Was our pastor somehow telling us that we shouldn't attend a Lutheran church because they were "imperfect"? Or was he saying that Lutherans were imperfect while the Reformed were perfect? The first question confused me. The latter irked me. I shared this with Bobby and he wondered to me if our pastor thought only the Reformed are perfect? We then joked that there is no perfect church because we would be attending.

The following Sunday we both felt well and the weather was perfect. The snow had melted, the ice had broken up and streamed down the curbs, and we could finally travel without feeling the highway was dangerous. However, that phone call providentially redirected us to attend Faith Lutheran again. It just bothered us that the pastor in Boise felt our Lutheran brethren were somehow second-class Christians. We walked into Bible study this time and enjoyed hearing those around us answering questions, reading the texts, and interacting with the Sunday school lesson for the day. We were warmly welcomed and pastor spoke with us again a little more at length.

The next week, Bobby was having surgery on his foot so we had shared this with some at church. On the morning of the surgery the doctor had called in the prescriptions for pain and antibiotic medicines. While I was at Wal-Mart, two of the ladies from church spotted me and immediately asked if Bobby had the surgery already and then prayed with me. Wow! Was this a benefit of attending a church closer to home, that I would meet fellow members at stores in town? Having attended a church 50+ miles away, this did not happen. The joy just overwhelmed me as I shared this with Bobby after his surgery was finished.

That week we decided we would try out the Wednesday Bible study at Faith Lutheran. When we arrived, the pastor gave us a binder with their study, which they had been working on for about a year already: *The Reformation and Reformers*. We both love church history and all things reformational and were excited to learn. Once again we heard of the work of God: how He does all things regarding our salvation; of justification by faith alone through grace alone; of the sacraments; of how many in the reformation would begin denying the presence of Christ in the true body and blood of the sacrament, denying that baptism actually does something, i.e., forgives us of our sins and washes us clean. I thought I knew Reformation history but over the next several months I was learning more and more and the scriptural teachings were becoming clearer each day.

To be honest, we haven't stopped learning. As I attend the ladies Bible study, I find that I am seeing things plainly written in the Word that either I'd just skipped over, or worse, tried to reinterpret them while doing some mental and theological gymnastics. Reading from *Concordia*, the *Lutheran Service Book*, and *Luther's Small Catechism*, we can say we have found the church which has maintained the true teachings of Christ and remained steadfast and faithful by God's grace.

One aspect of Lutheran dogmatics, which I greatly appreciate, is that when you read the Bible you read it for what it actually says. When we see something that might be contradictory we recognize that, as my dear friend says, "God is a lot smarter than us." Truly, reading the word of God plainly, simply, with recognition that *is* means *is*, *all* means *all*, the warnings are real and baptism actually saves, has removed from my own mind and heart the burden I laid upon myself to figure out God. When reading the debate between Dr. Theodore Beza, of Geneva (Reformed) and Dr. Jakob Andreae (Lutheran) at the Colloquy of Montbâeliard, I came across this quote from Dr. Osiander:

> *If you always make sport of all the plain testimonies of Holy Scripture after this fashion through interpretations, what will we have for certain in the whole of Holy Scripture left at the end? For example: Simon (the magician) believed, that is, he pretended to believe.*[2]

2. Andreae and Armstrong, *Lutheranism Vs. Calvinism*, 537.

In Lutheranism we have found a faith that is vibrant and alive, serving God and neighbor. Far from perfect, we have ended up in quite the perfectly-imperfect church and are growing, living, and loving Christ, His church, and our neighbors.

CHAPTER 2

Lutheran Undercurrents

As my husband and I were reforming, we were told by Lutheran friends and ministers that we were "more *Lutheran* than Reformed." There seemed to always be these Lutheran undercurrents in our understanding of the Scripture. We were "sort of Lutheran" without even knowing it. In 2005, I went back to college to earn my bachelors degree. The intent was to become a Christian counselor and so I set out on a new adventure. However, my first professor, Dr. John Warwick Montgomery, a Lutheran, impacted me greatly to change my concentration from biblical counseling to theology with an emphasis on apologetics. So began my instruction in a Lutheran defense of the faith and the beginning of God reforming both me and my husband's theology to reflect that of the reformers. This was going to be some theological ride and as a dear friend once said, he had "never seen two people reform so quickly." Much of what we believed did reflect that of Scripture and turned out was more Reformed than modern evangelicalism but often just a bit too "Lutheran" for the Reformed to agree.

Later that year, during summer vacation, God had providentially given us both two books to read: *God's Generals II* and *Old Paths*. As we read those books we each realized that the type of salvation teaching we had been under for all of our Christian lives was a works-based, enthusiast type of Christianity. God began to teach us through His Word and through the writings of others about the true faith, especially about justification by faith alone. Soon we were reading widely from various reformers but none more than Luther himself. We left our evangelical charismatic church and sought out a Reformed church in our neighborhood. Little by little we were learning the true gospel. However, issues soon arose in the local church and we decided to leave.

We were beside ourselves when we left because the circumstances were devastating. Not knowing where to go, and others from the local church literally showing up on our doorstep the following Sunday, Bobby, an ordained minister with the International Assemblies of God at the time, gave in to the call to lead this band of "misfits" as we came to call ourselves (referencing the Island of Misfit Toys from *Rudolph the Red-Nosed Reindeer*). We and a handful of other believers began to study together the Five Solas of the Reformation and soon learned that we neither do work to become a Christian nor to stay one. As our little band of misfits grew we came under the oversight of two Navy-men, one a chaplain, the other studying to become a minister. These two men would guide us in the development of the service and also check Bobby's sermons to make sure they followed the pattern of law and gospel. Gradually over time we became more and more Reformed in theology and practice.

These men influenced us greatly and often, when questioned by other Dutch or Presbyterian Reformed folks about what we believed, we would be told, "You're more Lutheran than Dutch." I suppose that was correct to some extent but we had a lot to learn and a lot more growing pains to endure. Still the seeds were planted; two of them specifically, which I will endeavor to discuss in more detail in the chapters ahead. But for now, they were: the Lord's Supper and baptism.

Since my time in the 1990s as a missionary with Wycliffe Bible Translators, I was exposed to other views of the Lord's Supper and whenever I partook of the elements my mind would be thinking, there is something more than just the bread and wine. When I began to learn the Heidelberg Catechism it did speak of the bread and wine being much more than a memorial but it still wasn't a settled issue in my mind or heart. As I worked on my dissertation, taking it from a Dutch Reformed perspective, I had to read a lot of the early works of the Dutch Reformers. I soon learned that the prince of Heidelberg had converted from Roman Catholicism to Lutheranism, to the disdain of his father. However, after hearing from some Swiss and French reformers, he spent about 30 days in a locked room to discern what the Lord's Supper actually was. Using only Scripture, but highly influenced by the Swiss Reformers and Calvin, he came to a logical deduction and realized that while it is more than bread and wine, it is not the true body and blood of our Lord Jesus Christ as the Lutherans and ancient church believed and taught. That never sat well in my heart. This way of interpreting the Scriptures had a hint of enthusiasm and Gnosticism. The prince was figuring it out logically and on his own. However, since that was not my focus in my dissertation, it was shelved in my mind until a later date.

This teaching on the Lord's Supper would become one of the key reasons we converted to Lutheranism. The Lord's Supper was one major part of what I was missing during the harsh winter. I was spiritually starving and longed to be fed on the true body and blood of our Lord. This was not the correct Dutch Reformed view of this, and I knew it, but it was what I was sensing while we were kept away from Boise during the winter months.

As to baptism and that it actually does work forgiveness (1 Peter 3:21, baptism now saves) was also shocking to me. I grew up Pentecostal and traveled to Heidelberg theologically and never thought about the text in 1 Peter, or any of the others, which point to baptism being the means through which God actually washes away our sins. In the Pentecostal and evangelical churches we were simply taught that baptism was our response to God and our testimony to the world that we were going to follow Jesus. In the Dutch Reformed churches, though viewed as a sacrament, it still did not actually do anything except mark that infant, child, or adult as part of the external community of believers. It did not work forgiveness in that person.

So, what brought me to Lutheranism? A harsh winter, hunger for the Lord's Supper, law and gospel preaching, and real fellowship with those of like faith. Primarily, it was two key teachings: Lord's Supper and baptism. I remember years back talking with a friend who was converting to Lutheranism and telling her that the Heidelberg teaches the same thing. Well, in all honesty, now that I know the teachings of the Book of Concord, she was right; they do not teach the same thing regarding the means of grace. In fact, the Dutch Reformed do not have the same views of these two sacraments. It is in the next few chapters I hope to share those teachings and how explosive they were in my heart and mind, how they connected all the pieces and settled the question of whether or not I have true faith in our Lord Jesus Christ.

Again, let me reiterate that at this point in my life, struggling with assurance, looking at my fruit and realizing that the spiritual fruit (Gal 6) in me was deformed, unripe, small and frail, I was a spiritual mess. I longed for an answer to my doubts and struggles. Little did I know they would come from Wittenberg and the Scriptures instead Heidelberg.

It is very interesting that neither I nor my husband realized that our own views of the Lord's Supper would be the catalyst which would bring us to a surer knowledge of God nor bring us out of Heidelberg and into Wittenberg. While it was not our intention to become Lutherans it was God's providential directing of the weather here in Idaho that made us *Accidental Lutherans.*

> *Hoc Est Corpus Meum—This Is My Body*
> *—Luther to Zwingli*

> *Baptism, which corresponds to this, now saves you . . .*
> *(1 Peter 3:21)*

Chapter 3

Something More

Hoc Est Corpus Meum

This Is My Body.

—LUTHER TO ZWINGLI,
AT THE COLLOQUY OF MONTBELIARD

A Nagging Question

THROUGHOUT MY CHRISTIAN LIFE I have had moments where I thought, these elements of the Lord's Supper are more than what they appear. It was deep within my heart and in my mind that would not be shaken; something more is here at the Lord's table, something more than a memorial or symbol. The very first time I participated in the Lord's Supper, when I heard the words, "Take, eat, this is my Body . . . take, drink, this is my blood . . ." I knew this was something more than a symbolic meal or a representation of the sufferings of my Lord and Savior Jesus Christ. This "something more" would nag at me for the next few decades not being settled until I believed what Jesus said, simply as He said it, "This is *My Body* . . . This is *My Blood* for the forgiveness of your sins."

Nothing more?

Typical of Baptist churches of all types, the matzos and grape juice were simply emblems of the body and blood of Christ. Baptists consistently declare that baptism and the Lord's Supper are symbols and are not necessary for salvation[1]. While solemn moments, especially in the Pentecostal church as they only served it when the pastor was told to by the Holy Spirit (this is a whole other topic to write about but I won't do that in this book), the elements of the Supper were never viewed as salvific or as a means of grace. In fact, until I became Reformed, I'd never even heard the phrase, means of grace.

As a Baptist, of a type, the elements were only bread and grape juice (we didn't use wine because you weren't supposed to get drunk . . . or even drink for that matter). They were simply reminders of what Jesus had done in the past and we ate and drank to simply obey Jesus' command that we do so in order to remember His sacrifice. As a believer there was nothing more to it. We wouldn't dare hold that it was more because, well, that was "too catholic" as in Roman Catholic. No! God forbid that you thought it was anything more than unleavened crackers or juice. That was forbidden.

As I reflect upon this, the Lord's Supper for the Baptist is nothing more than a memorial like the Washington or Lincoln memorials. They are simply pictures of the person they project and nothing more. Just as those monuments of marble and granite can do nothing more than mark out a spot, offer a plaque with information of the person, so, in the Baptist version of the Lord's Supper, the elements do nothing. They barely even feed a person on natural elements and certainly do not feed the believer spiritually except, perhaps, in some otherworldly manner as they think about what Jesus did and who He is. There is no nourishment, no grace, and no true help for the believer in these empty elements vacuous of Christ Himself.

1. Baptist Distinctives, "Baptists' Two Ordinances."

In partaking of the bread and the cup, Christ's disciples are to remember his sacrifice on the cross of Calvary as he gave his body and shed his blood for our sins. Baptists believe the Bible teaches that the elements used in the Supper are not literally the body and blood of Christ.

> They are symbols of his body and blood. In eating the bread and drinking from the cup, a person does not actually partake of Christ's flesh and blood. Rather it is an opportunity to obey a command of Christ and to recall his sacrifice for us, his presence with us and his certain return.[2]

An Ordinance—The Lord's Supper as Law

Notice carefully how the gospel, the good news that Christ has come, lived, died and rose again for sinners, becomes a command in the Baptist view of the Lord's Supper. There is a muddying of the distinctive between law and gospel. Instead of the Lord's Supper being a "true celebration,"[3] a feast, a final gift of Christ to His disciples and to the church, the Baptist view is that this is a command. Instead of gospel, the Baptist view on the Lord's Supper is one of law or ordinance.

Having grown up in New York City, I am quite familiar with local ordinances. We had laws about parking on certain sides of the street, alternate side parking, and if you could not park you had to drive around until a spot opened or the ordinance changed and you could finally park on that side of the street. There were ordinances about restaurants and adding salt, or placing a salt shaker on the table. Later there were ordinances about what types of oil one could use to fry up some food and even the size cup one could purchase at local stores. Ordinances are laws. There is no getting around the definition of an ordinance no matter how the Reformed Baptists may want to change the definition; an ordinance is still a law. According Merriam-Webster an ordinance is "an authoritative

2. Baptist Distinctives, "Baptists' Two Ordinances."

3. Wieting, *Lutheranism 101: The Lord's Supper*, 25.

decree or direction; a law set forth by a governmental authority; prescribed usage, practice or ceremony . . ."[4] No matter how London Baptists may try to say differently, to call the Lord's Supper an ordinance is to call it a law.

That is the term the Reformed Baptist uses for the Lord's Supper as well as baptism. It is, for them, an act of obedience to partake of the bread and the cup but it does not impart to the believer anything of spiritual good. Rather, believers obey a command of Christ to recall His sacrifice and nothing more. To believe that the elements were the true body and true blood of Jesus would be denied and rejected and then offender probably brought swiftly to the pastor for correction. Also, for Baptists, they view the "juice from crushed grapes"[5] which symbolize that Christ shed his blood for us but they will not use fermented grapes . . . err, wine. Though Baptists hold that they are important because they were given to the church by Christ, nevertheless they help us to proclaim that gospel and nothing more. The Supper may move us and encourage us along the path of sanctification but it gives us no power, no grace by which that can actually be done. The Lord's Supper is also an opportunity to say thanks to Christ for His sacrifice and can be very special for the believer. Often, this was a time where I reflected upon the great sacrifice Jesus paid for my sins but it always left me wanting more and still feeling hungry for something more. What that was I did not know until I became Lutheran.

For the Reformed Baptist, their own teaching document, known as the 1689 London Baptist Confession of Faith, states that the Lord's Supper is what believers do in obedience to the command of Christ. It is "to be a bond and pledge of their communion with him, and with each other.[6]" A "memorial of that one offering up of himself . . . [7]" and not for the remission of sin or to impart grace. Though they were to be prayed over by the pastor and/or elders so that this bread and cup were to be "set apart

4. Merriam Webster Dictionary, "Ordinance."

5. Baptist Distinctives, "Baptists' Two Ordinances."

6. London Baptist Confession of Faith, "Chapter 30."

7. London Baptist Confession of Faith, "Chapter 30."

from a common to a holy use . . . [8]" In other words, they are still only figurative of Christ's body and blood and their substance and nature did not change, they remained *only* bread and juice or wine. The celebration of the Lord's Supper is something Christians are to do in obedience to Christ's command to "do this in remembrance of me . . ." and is actually called an "ordinance," a law. There is no grace in the Lord's Supper.

As Bobby and I meandered through the quagmire which is Reformed Baptist, we began to become very disheartened by the emphasis, not only in the Lord's Supper but also on the law and how great a place it took even within the preaching of sermons and writings of books and blogs and videos. Over and over we heard the law of God so that we would know what God requires of us, so that we would know we were sinners. Then, when we came to the table it was more law: "Do this because I command it. There's nothing to truly feed you on, but you have to do it to remember what I've done." Was it a special time? Yes. Many within the Reformed Baptists would remind us that it is the feast for the children of the kingdom and they did, rightfully, "fence the table," but it did not offer the believer anything but a memory. In the Baptist view (aka Zwinglian view) the Lord's Supper is nothing more than a picture and memorial. So often I would walk out of a church service feeling truly hungry for Christ. I'd heard the sermon, ate the bread and drank from the cup and yet, deep inside, I was starving for more. In my heart, I knew the Lord's Supper was *something more.*

Heidelberg vs. Wittenberg

The Heidelberg Catechism has much to say about the Lord's Supper. This catechism was commissioned by Frederick III of the Palatinate who is referred to as both a Philippist Lutheran (meaning they held to Philip Melanchthon's unapproved or authorized revision of the Augsburg Confession) and a latent Crypto-Calvinist (Crypto-Calvinists were German members of the Lutheran church

8. London Baptist Confession of Faith, "Chapter 30."

accused of secretly subscribing to Calvinist doctrine of the Eucharist in the decades immediately after the death of Martin Luther in 1546[9]). Both of these positions evidence that though Frederick III had converted to Lutheranism under the encouragement of his wife, Maria, princess of Brandenburg-Kulmback, he did not hold to the official Lutheran view as stated in both Martin Luther's catechism statements on the Lord's Supper. Prince Frederick III also rejected the authorized Augsburg Confession, instead adhering to the Variata, or the Revised Augsburg Confession of 1540 which Philip Melanchthon altered without authority from the princes who signed the original.[10]

Prince Frederick III, in order to determine which teaching on the Lord's Supper was biblical, spent approximately 30 days in a locked room to discern and determine what Jesus *really* meant by "This is my body . . . This is my blood." He came out, having great influence from both Calvin and Melanchthon in the past, believing Jesus did not mean "this is My Body . . . this is My Blood" but instead that it was a symbol and spiritual feeding only.

Here is what the Heidelberg Catechism teaches:

9. "Crypto-Calvinists." https://en.wikipedia.org/wiki/Crypto-Calvinism.

10. Almodovar, *Faith Seeking Unspeakable Consolation*, 163–64.

75.	Q.	How does the Lord's Supper signify and seal to you that you share in Christ's one sacrifice on the cross and in all his gifts?
	A.	In this way: Christ has commanded me and all believers to eat of this broken bread and drink of this cup in remembrance of him. With this command he gave these promises: First, as surely as I see with my eyes the bread of the Lord broken for me and the cup given to me, so surely was his body offered for me and his blood poured out for me on the cross. Second, as surely as I receive from the hand of the minister and taste with my mouth the bread and the cup of the Lord as sure signs of Christ's body and blood, so surely does he himself nourish and refresh my soul to everlasting life with his crucified body and shed blood.
776.	Q.	What does it mean to eat the crucified body of Christ and to drink his shed blood?
	A.	First, to accept with a believing heart all the suffering and the death of Christ, and so receive forgiveness of sins and life eternal. Second, to be united more and more to his sacred body through the Holy Spirit, who lives both in Christ and in us. Therefore, although Christ is in heaven and we are on earth, yet we are flesh of his flesh and bone of his bones, and we forever live and are governed by one Spirit, as the members of our body are by one soul.

777.	Q.	Are then the bread and wine changed into the real body and blood of Christ?
	A.	No. Just as the water of baptism is not changed into the blood of Christ and is not the washing away of sins itself but is simply God's sign and pledge, so also the bread in the Lord's Supper does not become the body of Christ itself, although it is called Christ's body in keeping with the nature and usage of sacraments.
778.	Q.	Why then does Christ call the bread his body and the cup his blood, or the new covenant in his blood, and why does Paul speak of a participation in the body and blood of Christ?
	A.	Christ speaks in this way for a good reason: He wants to teach us by his supper that as bread and wine sustain us in this temporal life, so his crucified body and shed blood are true food and drink for our souls to eternal life. But, even more important, he wants to assure us by this visible sign and pledge, first, that through the working of the Holy Spirit we share in his true body and blood as surely as we receive with our mouth these holy signs in remembrance of him, and, second, that all his suffering and obedience are as certainly ours as if we personally had suffered and paid for our sins.[11]

Brought up to Heaven?

It is only *spiritual* bread and wine. This now was giving me something more than just a memorial and symbolism. In the Reformed view the Lord's Supper was something more, it was a spiritual feeding. Believers were being fed spiritually on Christ. How? Well, in

11. "Lord's Day 28." http://www.heidelberg-catechism.com/en/lords-days/28.html

a strange way, when a believer partook of the elements they were spiritually lifted to where Christ is: heaven.

The Calvinist and Zwingli view is that the institution of the Lord's Supper, the words "This is my body . . . this is my blood," are spiritual. In actuality, these mean nothing other than that the spirit of Christ or the power of Christ's absent body is what is present but the true body and true blood are not present. "They pretend that they also believe a true presence of the true essential living body and blood of Christ in the holy supper however they say that this happens spiritually through faith."[12] In reality, both the Zwinglians and Calvinists may state that the body and blood are spiritually present, nevertheless they deny that the true blood and true body are present in, with, and under the bread.

The Calvinists or Reformed say that we should elevate ourselves into heaven by our thoughts through our faith and that in heaven is where we should seek Christ's body and blood. They deny that Christ is truly present because they believe that Christ, since his resurrection in his glorified body, can only be in one place at one time. Honestly, I barely knew this was the position of the Dutch Reformed as I don't think it was ever fully explained. Yet as I researched I found more and more Reformed and Presbyterian ministers teaching that in the Lord's Supper the believer is brought up to heaven, spiritually, and partakes of Christ that way. Huh? Not to sound harsh, but the charismatic often spoke of "trips to heaven."[13] This had to be a misunderstanding on my part. So, I researched more.

Rev. Gunn, a Presbyterian minister explains Calvin's view, that we are brought up to heaven and fed spiritually when he wrote,

> According to this view, the bread and wine represent the body and blood of Jesus. They do not in any way become the literal body and blood themselves . . . when we partake of the Lord's Supper, the Holy Spirit uses the symbolic message that Jesus is our spiritual nourishment,

12. Dau, *Concordia*, 488.

13. One example is *Heaven: Close Encounters of the God Kind* by Jesse Duplantis (Harrison House, 1996).

> to strengthen our faith in Jesus . . . The Holy Spirit accomplishes this is a way beyond our understanding, not through Jesus' coming down to earth at this time, but through our mystically ascending to heaven.[14]

In the Reformed view, the believer is brought up to Christ to have "real communion with Christ in heaven . . ." Since Christ's body is localized in heaven and He, in his glorified state, is not omnipresent, it is impossible for Christ to be present with us here on earth. The mystical union between believer and Christ is so connected that the Spirit of God uses the Lord's Supper to increase, confirm, and strengthen our faith, and in a "genuine sense" the Christian is now where Christ is, that is, in heaven.

In Calvin's *Institutes* he clarifies that the Lord's Supper is a sacrament, "a visible sign of a sacred thing" and that it is also a "visible Word of God" and is given to believers as a sign (symbol) of the promises of God only for those who in true faith, believing the gospel, partake of the elements.[15] He consistently connects it with the mystical union believers have in Christ. Accordingly, Calvin rejects that Christ is actually present but is rather spiritually present, yet it is the believer who is brought to heaven, not Christ to earth. Calvin argues along with the Baptist that when Jesus said, "This is my body" it is "the name of the thing signified ("body") applied to the sign (the bread) . . ." not the actually true body of Christ. For the Reformed, whether Presbyterian or Dutch, Calvinists hold to explaining what Jesus meant and reject what Jesus actually said. They believe that the Holy Spirit accomplishes in the spirit what is only signified in the earthly meal. Calvin would call this a spiritual eating which meant that by faith believers partake of the body and blood through the power of the Spirit but they were not actually eating and drinking the body and blood of the Lord Jesus Christ.

The writers of the Heidelberg Catechism also rejected that Christ was actually present, as Lutherans say it, in, with, and under

14. "Four Views of the Lord's Supper."

15. Calvin, *Calvin: Institutes*, loc. 31253, Kindle.

the bread and wine. Ursinus, the main writer of the Heidelberg Catechism, says in his commentary,

> The eating of the body, and the drinking of the blood of Christ is not corporal, but spiritual and embraces, 1. Faith in his sufferings and death, 2. The forgiveness of sins, and the gift of eternal life through faith. 3. Our union with Christ through the Holy Spirit who dwells both in Christ and in us. 4. The quickening influence of the same Spirit.[16]

Ursinus continues that we are to not take the Lord's words for simply what He said, *This* is my Body . . . *This* is my Blood. Rather, he calls a direct and simple understanding of what Jesus said as "absurd."[17] What Jesus meant to say is that it is a sign of his body and Jesus is just using a figure of speech. Further, Ursinus writes that the bread and wine are a sign but there is no union of the body of Christ with the bread and signifies the promise only to those who truly believe. When the Lord's Supper is received it is solely as a reminder of what Jesus did in dying for them and so they are to recall the benefits of salvation but the promise of Jesus "for the forgiveness of your sins" is not given but merely reiterated. It is up to the person to remember the effects of salvation and not to receive anything in the Lord's Supper.

In Question 78, the Heidelberg Catechism outright states that Calvinists and Dutch Reformed do not believe that Jesus' words, "this is my body . . ." actually mean what He said. Rather, the bread remains bread, the wine remains wine only. Yet, Jesus said, *This* is my Body. As Luther wrote on the table at the Castle of Marburg in the debate (colloquy), with Zwingli, "*hoc est corpus meum.*" Ursinus explains that Jesus was using a form of words and the bread and wine were symbols but not joined to that which they signified at all. The Reformed continue to say that Jesus was using a metonymy. In other words, Jesus was only using symbolic language and not speaking of reality. So, for the Reformed, the bread and wine are both a memorial, like the Baptists, and a sign which signifies

16. Ursinus, *Commentary on the Heidelberg Catechism*, location 21829.

17. "Four Views of the Lord's Supper."

Christ's body and blood but do not actually mean what Jesus said about them, *Hoc est corpus meum*. In the Reformed/Calvinist view, while they held it to be a sacrament they did not believe it to be a means of grace nor the true body and blood. To the Calvinist, this sign and seal was nothing more than a vacuous sacrament, a sign with no actual offering of grace or forgiveness of sins.

Somehow, even when I walked the roads of theology under the Heidelberg system, this never quite sat right with me. If Jesus meant it was a picture or symbol of His body and blood, then why didn't He just come out and say it? Certainly that clarity would have settled the debates between the reforming churches in Europe in the sixteenth century and done away with Zwingli's view of it being only a memorial or picture. If the bread was just bread, the wine just wine, why did Jesus say this, *this*, *this*, is my body . . . this, *this*, *this* is my blood? Somehow in this sacrament there just had to be something more.

The Lutheran View of Something More

Something more . . . there just had to be something more to the Lord's Supper than an empty memorial or a vacuous sacrament. If it was only a picture of the death and sacrifice of Jesus upon the cross then it didn't matter how often we partook. However, if the early church in Acts was partaking each time they came together for worship then could there be something more?

In his homily to the people of Antioch, St. Chrysostom says that if we do not rightly take the Lord's Supper, then, "you also be guilty of the body and blood of Christ."[18] If the early church believed that the bread and wine in the Lord's Supper was actually Christ's true body and true blood then this concept that it is merely a memorial or a symbol. Then this becomes a new idea. The ancient church held to our Lord's words exactly as he said them, "this is my body . . . this is my blood." In *Lutheranism 101* on the Lord's Supper, the author writes "true those same 16 centuries,

18. Chrysostom, "Homily 60 on Matthew."

there is no record of the church of Christ gathering for worship on the Lord's day and not having the opportunity to receive the New Testament of Christ's body and blood."[19]

The question then becomes, What does the Bible say? The pattern in this book has been to write out what the Baptists believed, then what the Reformed believed, then the Lutherans, and then Scripture. Yet, as I study more and more about the Lord's Supper (as well as other teachings, i.e., baptism) it becomes much more evident that by delineating the Lutheran view and the scriptural, that it will be repetitive. What you will see is that the Lutherans simply take the words of Jesus as he said them. Yet, Baptists or various Reformed outlooks and interpretations of Jesus' words of institution try to explain away the actual words. They hold that Jesus did not mean what He plainly said but instead meant the bread and wine are symbols or pictures of His body and blood. The Reformed look at this and say there is spiritual nourishment here yet it is not the true body and true blood of Jesus Christ. The Lutherans read the Scriptures which say "this is my body, this is my blood" and simply say this is his body, this is his blood. They do not add or subtract from what Jesus says. Lutherans simply take Jesus' words for what they mean.

A great question, which one can find in *Lutheranism 101: The Lord's Supper* is this:

> *If Jesus did not mean this Bread and this Wine is His True Body and True Blood, then what would He have said if He did mean the Bread and Wine are His Body and Blood?*[20]

In other words, what could Jesus have said differently to tell us this bread is my body broken for you . . . or . . . this wine is my blood shed for the forgiveness of your sins? In Luther's small catechism the first question is, what is the sacrament of the altar?

Luther writes, "It is the true body and blood of our Lord Jesus Christ under the bread and wine, instituted by Christ himself for us Christians to eat and to drink." The second question is so

19. Wieting, *Lutheranism 101: The Lord's Supper*, 26.

20. Wieting, *Lutheranism 101: The Lord's Supper*, 26.

important because it tells us what the Scriptures say and by that what Lutherans believe:

> Where is this written? The holy evangelists Matthew, Mark, Luke, and St. Paul right:
>
> Our Lord Jesus Christ, on the night when he was betrayed, took bread and when he had given thanks, he broke it and gave it to the disciples and said: "Take, eat; this is my body, which is given for you. This do in remembrance of me."
>
> In the same way also he took the cup after supper, and when he had given thanks, he gave it to them, saying, "Drink of it, all of you; this cup is the New Testament in my blood, which is shed for you for the forgiveness of sins. This do, is often as you drink it, in remembrance of me."[21]

The words of Christ in the Lord's Supper cannot be separated from the gifts they give. The Lord's Supper is given to us as Jesus said for the forgiveness of sins. These gifts—forgiveness, cleansing, washing, renewing—that our wise Christ has given through the words of institution and, in the Lord's Supper, the Bible, are clear. Jesus said this as he handed the disciples the bread: "this bread is my body." Then when Jesus handed them the cup, he said, "this cup is the forgiveness of sins this is my blood, shed for you for the forgiveness of sins." Without trying to jump through hoops, or what I have called *theological gymnastics*, we must simply take what Jesus said as truth.

Enigma and Riddle of Faith

The traditional complaint against the biblical words that Jesus used is that He could not possibly have meant that when we eat the bread and drink from the cup that he really and truly meant that we were eating his body and drinking his blood. Surely that is not what Jesus meant. How could that be? Proceeding to the article of the Lord's Supper, Luther cut right to the chase, saying:

21. Luther, *Luther's Small Catechism*, 322.

> I do not ask how Christ can be God and man, and how his natures could be united. For God is able to act far beyond our imagination. To the word of God one must yield. It is up to you to prove that the body of Christ is not there when Christ himself says, 'This is my body.' I do not want to hear what reason says. I completely reject carnal or geometrical arguments, as for example, that a large body could not fill a small space. God is above and beyond all mathematics, and his words are to be adored and observed with awe. God, however, commands: 'Take, eat; this is my body'. I request, therefore, a valid proof from Holy Writ that these words do not mean what they say.[22]

At this point Luther then wrote the words "This is my body" (*hoc est corpus meum*) on the table with chalk, placing the tablecloth over it. From the plain meaning of these words he would not budge.[23]

> Luther said, (God) hides Himself in the enigma and riddle of faith that God is an incomprehensible God. Even in the mystery of incarnation, where we can know him, he remains hidden in his humanity. He is hidden in the church, as he is in the sacrament of the Eucharist, where he is 'most hidden'.[24]

Marburg Colloquy: Showdown between Scripture and Human Philosophy

The discussion between what the Scriptures said in the institution of the Lord's Supper and what the mind could fathom and therefore engaged human philosophy (Thomist in particular) came down to a colloquy at the Castle of Marburg on October 1–4, 1529 between

22. Stephen Preus, "The Marburg Colloquy." https://lutheranreformation.org/history/the-marburg-colloquy/.

23. Stephen Preus, "The Marburg Colloquy." https://lutheranreformation.org/history/the-marburg-colloquy/.

24. Sasse, *This Is My Body*, 118.

Zwingli and Oecolampadius. Did Jesus mean what he said at the Last Supper as recorded in the Gospels and St. Paul? Luther, it is recorded by Melanchthon, in a private discussion with Oecolampadius stood by his position and told him, "God said, This is my body. God is omnipotent. Consequently the body is in the bread."[25]

Zwingli would ask over and over, "What is the use of such eating?" Luther's answer is: "It is not our business to ask and to answer such questions. If Christ instituted the sacrament and told us, 'This is my body,' we are to obey His commandment and believe His words."[26] Luther refused to attempt to figure God out, how He works in and through the Sacraments. Luther would say, "We must leave that to the inscrutable wisdom of God."[27] Over and over again Luther would simply go to what the word of God said. Luther held strongly to reading God's word simply as it said. He did understand that there were times when Scripture used symbolism and metanomys but he said at Marburg that Zwingli and Oecolampadius would have to prove that Jesus was speaking in symbolism here, at the Last Supper, in that fashion.

In fact, Luther said that he didn't deny that there are cases of figurative speech in the Scriptures; however, he said to Zwingli,

> . . . still you have to prove that this is such a case. It is not enough that these words: this is my body, can be understood in that way. What you have to prove is that they must be understood figuratively. You want me to build the faith of my heart on this foundation. That means you are unwilling to produce any proof at all. Thus my faith is strengthened by your failure to give a proof. I have a clear and powerful text.[28]

Instead Luther actually made use of the traditional thoughts of the earlier church which regarded the sacrament of the altar as food and medicine. He quotes at Marburg from Irenaeus,

25. Sasse, *This Is My Body*, 118.
26. Sasse, *This Is My Body*, 181.
27. Sasse, *This Is My Body*, 181.
28. Sasse, *This Is My Body*, 233.

> . . . it is indeed called a food of souls which nourishes and strengthens the new man for my baptism we are firstborn anew; but . . . There still remains, besides, the old vicious nature of flesh and blood in may have, and there are so many hindrances and temptations of the devil and of the world that we often become weary in feeling and sometimes stumble. Therefore, it is given for a daily pastor and sustenance, that faith may refresh and strengthen itself so as not to fall back in such a battle but become even stronger and stronger with a new life must be so regulated that it may continually increase in progress.[29]

Luther was adamant that you must believe the words Jesus spoke; if he said about the bread, this is my body then this is the true body of our Lord Jesus Christ. If Jesus said this cup is for the forgiveness of sins, then forgiveness of sins is in, with, and under the cup. When Jesus called the cup the New Testament in his blood and spoke of the wine as his blood, he meant what he said. The ancient church looked at the sacrament of the altar as medicine for the soul. They didn't quibble over how Jesus is present in, with, and under the elements. They simply accepted it and so must we.

Martin Chemnitz in his work on the Lord's Supper writes,

> For what purpose in His supper as distributed in these elements to be received by the communicants and what is the salutary use or what is the spiritual benefit of those things we receive in the supper from Christ who distributes them? This point is treated in these words of the institution quote this do in remembrance of me" that is, remember that my body which you are receiving was given for you in the blood which you are drinking which shed for you for the remission of sins; and also in these words: this cup is the New Testament in my blood" these words do not speak of some historical, cold, or idle memory, but of true faith, which lays hold of and applies to itself Christ with all his merits and benefits for reconciliation, salvation, and eternal life.[30]

29. Sasse, *This Is My Body*, 182.

30. Chemnitz, *Chemnitz's Works*, 2.

In the ancient church, the Lord's Day Supper, a divine service, without the celebration of the Lord's Supper was inconceivable. In fact, in the very early years of the church the divine service was open to all. The view was so high, though, that the Lord's Supper was closed and was done behind doors to keep the un-baptized from participating. The supper was never for all those present. Rather, it was only for the baptized or later for the confirmed only. Participating in the body and blood was only for the one who was baptized and confirmed in Jesus Christ. Unlike the Anabaptists, Luther refused to throw out what the ancient church had held since Christ instituted the Supper. Many find it strange that Lutherans hold to what the ancient church proclaimed, namely, that Jesus meant what he said and there were no hidden meanings.

Lutherans believe Jesus spoke plainly, so plainly that it is quite simply *plain and simple* because it was the last supper. Think about this: when someone is dying and they give their deathbed testimony, the authorities receive that as true and binding. They don't go and look for hidden meanings in symbolism or pictures, monuments or memorials. Instead they take the words of that final testimony to mean what those words state. In the same way, when approaching God's word, where it is plainly written, we must not play semantics with God's word. What is plain is plain and the Lord's institution, or rather his words of institution, are plain and simple. I'm not saying it is simple to understand. However, what the church has said is that what Jesus said, his words, mean what they say.

> Everything depends on these words. Every Christian should and must know them and hold them fast. He must never let anyone take them away from him by any other kind of teaching, even though it were an angel from heaven. They are words of life and of salvation so that whoever believes in them has all his sins forgiven through that faith; he is a child of life and has overcome death and hell. Language cannot express how great and mighty these words are for they are the sum and substance of the whole gospel.[31]

31. Wieting, *Lutheranism 101: The Last Supper*, 26.

Why the warnings?

In the debate at Montbâeliard between Dr. Jacob Andreae and Theodore Beza, Dr. Beza took the view that when Jesus said the words "this is my body and that this is my blood" he was using a figurative or literary device. However, Dr. Andreae states that in the same way the Gospel writer wrote that the dove which descended upon Jesus Christ was the Holy Spirit in the form of a dove, it was not merely a sign of the Holy Spirit but was the Holy Spirit. There are many other places in Scripture in which the Lord does use figurative language. One such example is when Jesus says, I am the door. Yet, we do not take Jesus to mean he is a 6½-foot piece of wood with hinges placed within a doorframe. Then again when Jesus says he is the light, we must take that as he is the light because he says "I am the light of the world."

On the night that Jesus held his last supper, these were going to be his final words to his disciples. Surely a man who knows he is going to his death is not about to use figurative language or symbols of what he means. A dying man tells the truth in an unadulterated manner. A man about to go to his execution will speak clearly without metonyms, symbols, or figures. So when Jesus said to his disciples at this final meal, hours before his arrest, before his torture, before his crucifixion, that this bread is his body, this is his blood which is shed for you for the forgiveness of sins, then that is exactly what Jesus meant.

However, if the bread and wine of the Lord's Supper are simply bread and wine then why the warnings? When you visit a memorial, there are no warnings about visiting the memorial. You visit the Washington Monument, there is no threat from the Washington Monument against you. You visit the Lincoln Memorial, the Grand Canyon, or the Statue of Liberty, those things cannot harm you and therefore, there are no warnings. Yet, Paul tells us that if you eat in an unworthy manner you became sick and died. While we don't know necessarily how they became sick and died, the Scripture says they ate in an unworthy manner and therefore they became sick and died.

In 1 Corinthians 11 Paul writes,

> For I received from the Lord what I also delivered to you, that the Lord Jesus on the night when he was betrayed took bread, and when he is given thanks, he broke it, and said, "this is my body, which is for you. Do this in remembrance of me." In the same way he also took the cup, after supper, saying, "this cup is the new covenant in my blood. Do this, as often as you drink it, in remembrance of me." For as often as you eat this bread and drink the cup you proclaim the Lord's death until he comes.
>
> Whoever, therefore, eats the bread or drinks the cup of the Lord in an unworthy manner will be guilty concerning *the body and blood of the Lord.* Let a person examine themselves, then, and so eat of the bread and drink the cup. For anyone who eats and drinks *without discerning the body* eats and drinks judgment on himself and is why many of you are weak and ill, and some have died. (1 Cor. 11:23–30)

Notice that Paul says, in the parts that I've emphasized, "the body and blood of the Lord" and "without discerning the body." These are the questions which would run through my mind as I doubted the memorial view which I had been taught as a Baptist/ Pentecostal over and against the vacuous sacramental view of the Reformed which I was being taught through their Heidelberg Catechism. Once again my heart and mind would be conflicted as I longed for something more.

1. Why doesn't Paul say the bread and wine that symbolize our Lord?
2. Why doesn't he warn against eating bread and wine drinking alone but adds the body and blood of our Lord?
3. Paul warns that they haven't discerned the body of our Lord and because of that they are bringing judgment on themselves.
4. Why a warning if the elements are simply bread and wine?
5. Why does Paul tell us we have to discern the body?

6. Why is Paul telling us that if we take of the elements, eating the bread and drinking the cup, in an unworthy manner, we are guilty of the body and blood of the Lord?

These are questions that ran through my mind throughout my early Christian years. I wondered, why a warning? If it is just a picture, symbol, metonym, then why would people eating bread and wine risk severe judgment? As a Reformed believer it seemed to be a little clearer that we were participating in the body and blood of Christ; however, it was always that the true body of Christ could only be in one place, heaven, because he has body. We were taught that Christians, true believers could be raised in our faith up to heaven and participate in the body and blood of the Lord. However, that never sat quite right in my mind or heart.

In fact, many Reformed will tell you that in the holy supper Christ's body is truly received by believers and they will insist that they understand this presence of Christ's body and blood not as a presence here on earth or in, with, and under the elements but only with respect to faith. In other words, our faith is "reminded and excited by the visible signs . . . Its (our faith) elevates itself and ascends above all heavens it then receives and enjoys Christ's body, which is present there in heaven. Yes, they say they receive Christ himself, together with all his benefits, in a true and essential way, but nevertheless only in a spiritual way."[32] The Reformed held that the bread and wine here on earth not in heaven but Christ's body is now in heaven and so we elevate ourselves to heaven to participate in his blood and body. Yet in many ways even the Reformed held that the Lord's Supper was a sign and symbol or picture and not a true sacrament (for a true sacrament is that which works forgiveness of sins, actually doing that which it signifies).

Even in the Pentecostal church I grew up in, the charismatic church I later attended all the way through to the Reformed church that we were part of for over 12 years, prior to taking the Lord's Supper the minister would give the warning: "if you are not a

32. Formula, Solid Declaration, Article VII. The Holy Supper, Dau, *Concordia,* 563.

believer, if you have not repented and confessed your faith in Jesus Christ, we ask that you do not participate in the Lord's Supper but let the elements pass by you." Why? Why can't unbelievers partake of the Lord's Supper? After all, it is simply a symbol, a memorial, a metonymy. So, it must be something more.

Again Paul in 1 Corinthians says, "the cup of blessing that we bless, is it not a participation in the blood of Christ? The bread that we break, is it not a participation in the body of Christ?" (1 Cor. 10:16). Indeed Paul tells us that we are participating in the body and blood of Christ when we partake, eat, of the bread and wine. The early church guarded this carefully because they celebrated it. The church throughout the ages, up until the sixteenth century, participated in the body of Christ (via the bread), and the blood of Christ (via the wine). The early church believed the very words of Christ and did not try to explain them away. If, therefore, just the elements of the Lord's Supper are only bread and wine or simply a memorial, why the warnings?

Something More

The warnings are there because the bread and wine are something more than bread and wine. Scripture says it is the body and blood of Christ and therefore, we accept it. We do not try to figure it out. We do not try to put words in Jesus' mouth when the very words He spoke are simple enough to understand: *Hoc est corpus meum*. This is my body. As Lutherans we take Jesus' words to say what He meant and meant what He said.

So what are the benefits of taking the Lord's Supper? What are the benefits of taking the Lord's Supper? Luther answers that his small catechism on part six on the sacrament of the altar he says that it is shown us in these words, "given for you" and "shed for you for the forgiveness of sins."[33] This means that in the sacrament forgiveness of sins, life, and salvation are given us through

33. Luther, *Luther's Small Catechism*, 29.

these words, for where there is forgiveness of sins, there is also life and salvation.

Christ established this meal, this personal meal, this corporate meal for believers to celebrate one with another because he established by his own command that they convey his grace. They are not an empty ceremony or rite; rather this is a meal given to us by Christ by which he feeds us on his body and blood for the forgiveness of sins. In the sacrament, "we receive a great treasure: the forgiveness of sins.[34]" As believers we should be receiving the Lord's Supper regularly because in it Jesus has invited us to come, take, and eat—"this is my body"—and is actually giving us his true body and true blood. In, with, and under bread and wine, Christ Himself is given to us and strengthens us, forgives us, and encourages us, through His own self. He, in, with, and under the bread and wine, gives us what we need to serve others. It has often been said that baptism is the initiation sacrament which brings you into the body of Christ. In the Lord's Supper, however, that is where He rejuvenates our faith, strengthens our faith, forgives us of our sins, and cleanses us from all unrighteousness. The blood which He shed He gives to us in the cup or the forgiveness of sins. His true body which was broken for us He now gives to us in, with, and under the bread.

Each week in the divine service God first calls us to repent and then absolves us of our sins as our pastor gives us that absolution. We then hear from God through the preached word, the chanting of Psalms and hymns/songs, the readings of the Old Testament, the Epistles, and the Gospels. But each divine service culminates in Christ serving us his true body and true blood for the forgiveness of sins. Each week as I go up to the altar, kneel at the bar, and receive in the bread, the true body of my Lord and Savior Jesus Christ, and in the cup, the true blood of my Savior Jesus Christ, my heart sings as I hear the words from the pastor or the elders serving this body and this blood: "for you for the forgiveness of your sins." There can be no greater comfort than to know Jesus died for the world and because I am a part of the world and a

34. Luther, *Luther's Small Catechism*, 335.

sinner, Jesus died for me. When the pastor or elder says to me, "for you . . ." that assurance is bolstered. Whereas under the Reformed system I wondered whether or not I was among the elect, knowing that Jesus is the propitiation for the world (1 John 2:2) and that He gives me His true body and blood for the forgiveness of sins, I no longer have to wonder if Jesus died for me.

Though this is a very personal time of receiving from our Lord his true body and blood in, with, and under the bread and wine, nevertheless it is done corporately. Together we are served by Christ on His true body and true blood for the forgiveness of our sins. There on the altar, we the body of Christ receive the body and blood of Christ.

The Lord's Supper is indeed as Luther wrote "a gracious feast rather than an empty ceremony."[35] It is not simply . . .

> . . . the eating and the drinking, but the words of Christ together with his body and blood under the bread and wine that are the means through which forgiveness is bestowed. It is the joining of the eating and drinking of his true blood and body with faith that brings the blessings in touching Jesus and being touched by him and in faith receiving all the benefits he gives to us in his gracious feast.[36]

Luther taught that in those words "given and shed for you for the forgiveness of sins" that believers are to consider themselves and read themselves into the word *you*; it is for *you* for the forgiveness of your sins. Luther always reminds us that as the sacrament is for *you* it teaches us that Jesus Christ gave us this gracious feast because we are weak and struggling sinners; he feeds us on His true body and true blood to strengthen us and build up our faith. The eating and the drinking by us are not based upon how much faith we have in Him or our strength or how good we are. It is for sinners. It is through the true body and true blood in the bread and wine that we receive forgiveness of sins.

35. Luther, *Luther's Small Catechism*, 335.

36. Luther, *Luther's Small Catechism*, 335.

Often we were told in the Reformed especially that we had to prepare all week for the Lord's Supper so that we wouldn't eat or drink in an unworthy manner. Now that is an excellent practice to consider. We should be thinking all week long and on the Lord's day at the divine service where God serves us through absolution, through his preached word, through the Lord's Supper, and through those means of grace, which we are going to receive the forgiveness of sin and that our faith will be strengthened. However, as the Solid Declaration states, "We reject the teaching that worthiness comes not only from true faith, but also from a person's own preparation."[37] We don't prepare to make ourselves worthy. We are miserable sinners. Each of us struggles through the week. But on the Lord's day what a gracious feast awaits us at the table of our Lord where he serves us his own true body and true blood. "Whoever believes these words has exactly what they say: 'forgiveness of sins.'"[38]

Scripture Speaks

What I love about Lutherans is their approach to the teachings and doctrines of the church. When I would ask my pastor, "What is your view on such and such?" His answer was always, "Well, let's see what the Bible has to say about that." Isn't that wonderful? No more looking at man's opinion but rather looking into the word of God. So, let's see what the Bible has to say about the Lord's Supper by using the statement in *Luther's Small Catechism* to begin with:

> Where is this written? The holy evangelists Matthew, Mark, Luke, and St. Paul write:
>
> Our Lord Jesus Christ, on the night when he was betrayed, took bread and when he had given thanks, he broke it and gave it to the disciples and said: " take, eat; this is my body, which is given for you. This do in remembrance of me."

37. Formula, Solid Declaration Articles VII. The Holy Supper, Dau, *Concordia*, 563.

38. Luther, *Luther's Small Catechism*, 335.

> In the same way also he took the cup after supper, and when he had given thanks, he gave it to them, saying, "Drink of it, all of you; this cup is the New Testament in my blood, which is shed for you for the forgiveness of sins. This do, is often as you drink it, in remembrance of me."[39]

Hoc Est Corpus Meum (This is My Body)

In this section of the catechism, Martin Luther is bringing together all the statements from that night before Jesus' crucifixion into one paraphrased form. If we read it as Jesus spoke it, then we read, "This is my body . . . this is my blood." Jesus did not quantify his statement, saying, "this bread is a symbol of my body . . . this wine is a picture of my blood." Rather, Jesus said simply, "this (the bread) is my body . . . this (the wine, the cup) is my blood for the forgiveness of your sins." Simple. Straightforward. Unequivocally *this is*; Hoc Est. There was no adding of symbol, picture, memorial, or metonymy but a simple giving out of the element stating the bread is his body and the wine is His blood.

I have already gone through some of the verses which speak of the Lord's Supper, but it is good to read them again just as they are written.

> Is not the cup of blessing which we bless a sharing in the blood of Christ? Is not the bread which we break a sharing in the body of Christ? 1 Cor. 10:18
> Therefore whoever eats the bread or drinks the cup of the Lord in an unworthy manner, shall be guilty of the body and the blood of the Lord. For he who eats and drinks, eats and drinks judgment to himself if he does not judge the body rightly. For this reason many among you are weak and sick, and a number sleep. (1 Cor 11:27–32)

I ask you to read 1 Corinthians 10:18 again. Don't try to figure it out but read the text as Paul wrote it. What is he saying here? Well, not to repeat the apostle but he is saying, "Isn't the cup a

39. Luther, *Luther's Small Catechism*, 322.

sharing in the blood of Christ? Isn't the bread a sharing in the body of Christ?" Notice how he did not say, "Isn't the cup a symbol or memorial of the blood and of the Bread?" He says, emphatically, that they are the true body and true blood of our Lord and Savior Jesus Christ. Paul did not write that the bread and wine were symbolically pictures of Jesus and His sufferings; rather, he says that they are the body and blood of Jesus Christ.

Read it over and over. Paul, here, had the chance to clarify the Lord's Supper *if* it was only bread and wine that symbolized the body and blood. However, the apostle Paul did not. In fact, he warned against that view, stating that if you did not believe you were participating in the body and blood of our Lord and Savior, then you were at risk of sickness and even death. How does bread and wine do that? However, if you are eating the body and blood of Christ in an unworthy manner, rejecting that you are participating in the body and blood of Jesus Christ, then you are risking everything.

> Therefore whoever eats the bread or drinks the cup of the Lord in an unworthy manner, shall be *guilty of the body and the blood of the Lord*. For he who eats and drinks, eats and drinks judgment to himself if he does not judge the body rightly. *For this reason many among you are weak and sick, and a number sleep*. (1 Cor 11:27–32)

In 1 Corinthians 11, Paul warns us that there are those who do not discern the Lord's body rightly and because of that they are experiencing judgment from God. While no details are offered as to how this judgment is exhibited, the point is that they are not discerning the body and the blood and because of that eat it unworthily. By not believing the bread is the true body and the wine the true blood, those participating, or communing, are actually guilty of the body and blood. Paul connects the elements with Jesus Himself.

Now I understand this is hard to fathom. For a long time you have been taught that the bread and cup are just pictures of Jesus' body and blood. However, is that what the Bible actually says? Read these verses again from both the Gospel accounts and from Paul's writings. Read them without the explanations trying to figure out what Jesus said. Read them plainly, read them word for word, then tell yourself what Jesus said, "This is my body . . . This is my blood . . ." Exactly. See what they say? Jesus, had he meant symbol or picture surely would have added that in since this was a key moment in his life and ministry. He was about to be executed on the cross for the sins of the world and would not have muddied his terminology here. Rather, he would have said exactly what He meant and meant exactly what He said.

Lutherans state, "We believe, teach, and confess that the words of Christ's testament are not to be understood in any other way than the way they read, according to the letter. So the bread does not signify Christ's absent body and the wine His absent blood. But, because of the sacramental union, the bread and wine are truly Christ's Body and blood."[40]

As I grow in grace and knowledge, by God's mercy I am finding that what I had either dismissed as "Well, God could not really have meant that . . ." or "There's got to be a spiritual interpretation for this . . ." is now, Wow! God really did say that. I've learned too, that what Jesus says is important because you cannot sever the words of Christ from the gifts of His gospel and grace. Remove the reality of these words and you are left with an empty, vacuous picture that has no effect on the believer. If it is just bread and wine, one has to come back to the warnings of Scripture and by doing that one is confronted by the very Words of God and the realization that there is something more here than just bread and wine but that Jesus' true body and blood are given to you "for the forgiveness of your sins."

Luther was adamant, and so must we be, that we believe the words Jesus spoke. If he said about the bread, this is my body, then this is the true body of our Lord Jesus Christ. If Jesus said this cup is for the forgiveness of sins, then forgiveness of sins is in, with, and under the cup. When Jesus called the cup his blood and spoke of the wine as his blood, he meant what he said. The ancient church

40. Formula, Solid Declaration Article VII. The Holy Supper, in Dau, *Concordia*, 563.

looked at the sacrament of the altar as medicine for the soul. They didn't quibble over how Jesus is present in, with, and under the elements. They simply accepted it and so must we.

Martin Chemnitz in his work on the Lord's Supper writes,

> For what purpose in His supper as distributed in these elements to be received by the communicants and what is the salutary use or what is the spiritual benefit of those things we receive in the supper from Christ who distributes them? This point is treated in these words of the institution quote this do in remembrance of me" that is, remember that my body which you are receiving was given for you in the blood which you are drinking which shed for you for the remission of sins; and also in these words: this cup is the New Testament in my blood" these words do not speak of some historical , cold, or idle memory, but of true faith, which lays hold of and applies to itself Christ with all his merits and benefits for reconciliation, salvation, and eternal life.[41]

41. Chemnitz, *Chemnitz's Works*, 2.

Chapter 4

God's Own Child

The Forgiveness of Sins through the Waters of Baptism

These past two years what God did for me in baptism has become a precious teaching. It has brought comfort and assurance to know that all the blessings of the gospel, of salvation and the forgiveness of sins, were fully realized in the waters of baptism. There has been one dear friend, Lee Ann, who also grew up Baptist, with whom this comfort has been shared. Each week we would speak to each other about verses we had read dozens of times and now see that they were about baptism and how God does the regenerating, forgiving, and declaring us justified in Jesus Christ and that none of it is our work. In mid-week Bible study we were learning about the sacrament of baptism but also in our ladies' study we often came across the biblical teaching on this holy sacrament. Sometimes we would just look at each other knowingly that once again what we had been taught was either incomplete or simply wrong and how now assurance of salvation had come. At the time I am writing this, Lee Ann's cancer has come back and she will soon be home with her Savior Jesus Christ,[1] forever rejoicing and praising Him that she is *God's own child . . . and gladly says it.*

1. The Dorcas Women's Group was begun many years ago at Faith

(Today, January 29, 2019, I received a call that Lee Ann had been called home to be with her faithful and gracious Savior forever and ever. I will miss her greatly but our comfort and Lee Ann's is and was that in the waters of baptism, Christ had regenerated, forgiven, redeemed and given her true faith, and He sustained and kept her, nourishing her on His true body and blood. She now sees Him, whom she loved so much, face to face and is rejoicing with saints of all ages praising Him. I look forward to the day I am called home and will worship Him with all who have gone before me.)

God used Lee Ann, many times, to help me realize the blessings of our baptism and how God brought us to a more biblical understanding of the work He did for us even when we didn't understand it at the time. Often, when something became clear to us, we would just look at each other and smile. On Wednesday nights, our pastor would sometimes have us sing the following hymn ("God's Own Child," I'll gladly say it) and it has taken deep root in my heart. I thank God that He brought Lee Ann into my life and will miss her greatly. Still, come to my office when I am working and you will often hear this hymn playing in the background as I write or read:

> *God's own child, I gladly say it: I am baptized into Christ!*
> *He, because I could not pay it, gave my full redemption price.*
> *Do I need earth's treasures many? I have one worth more than any*
> *That brought me salvation free, Lasting to eternity!*

Lutheran in order to serve the local Mountain Home community, help with educational scholarships, support various ministries, etc. They have encouraged me to continue my academic pursuits, supporting me so that I may be better equipped for the task ahead.

Today, January 29, 2019, I received a call that Lee Ann had been called home to be with her faithful and gracious Savior forever and ever. I will miss her greatly but our comfort and hers is and was that in the waters of baptism Christ had regenerated, forgiven, redeemed her and given true faith in Christ Jesus our Lord and Savior and through the Lord's Supper, He fed and sustained her faith through the true body and blood of our Lord, in, with, and under the bread and wine.

Sin, disturb my soul no longer: I am baptized into Christ!
I have comfort even stronger: Jesus' cleansing sacrifice.
Should a guilty conscience seize me, since my baptism did release me
In a dear forgiving flood, sprinkling me with Jesus' blood?

Satan, hear this proclamation: I am baptized into Christ!
Drop your ugly accusation; I am not so soon enticed.
Now that to the font I've traveled, all your might has come unraveled,
And, against your tyranny, God, my Lord, unites with me!

Death, you cannot end my gladness: I am baptized into Christ!
When I die, I leave all sadness to inherit paradise!
Though I lie in dust and ashes faith's assurance brightly flashes:
Baptism has the strength divine to make life immortal mine.

There is nothing worth comparing to this lifelong comfort sure!
Open-eyed my grave is staring: Even there I'll sleep secure.
Though my flesh awaits its raising, still my soul continues praising:
I am baptized into Christ; I'm a child of paradise![2]

The final line of this great hymn, "I am baptized into Christ, I'm a child of paradise," is what reminds me daily that because of God's work, in and through the water and the word, I am a child of paradise. When Satan comes and accuses me, or my own conscience falls beneath the load and guilt of sin, I can remember that, not on the basis of my decision, a sinner's prayer or my own faith, I am a child of God. Rather, it is solely upon His promises found in the sure Word, "Baptism now saves you" (1 Pet 3:19–22).

This idea that in the waters of baptism there is actually forgiveness of sins and salvation was new to me. In my own personal struggles for assurance I never looked at the work of forgiveness and justification in my baptism. That is what Oneness Pentecostals

2. Lutheran Church Missouri Synod, *Lutheran Service Book*, 594.

believed; baptismal regeneration, and to say it was verboten (forbidden) is an understatement. However, if I honestly looked at my fruit, the fruits of the spirit listed in Galatians, I was a spiritual mess and those fruits were deformed, unripe, small, and frail. Quite frankly, after this harsh winter I was a spiritual mess. As mentor to so many women, I could not admit it to them, let alone myself. Soon spiritual depression began to descend on me and I sank into despair. I was so embarrassed that I did not even share my struggles with my husband. After all, I have two master's in theology and a doctorate in apologetics and theology. How can I struggle with whether or not I am saved? So often I would awake in the middle of the night with panic attacks, wondering if I should suddenly die, would I go to heaven? How could I be sure? How in the world could I possibly know for a fact, a verifiable fact, that I was truly saved and God's child when my faith was small and my fruit malformed?

One time, several years before, I'd awakened from sleep in terror. I had dreamed I was at the gates of heaven when God asked me why He should let me in. In that dream I tried to point to my fruit but they were rotten to the core. I awoke in a sweat with my heart racing, and prayed, Lord, forgive me. It was a hymn that came to mind where the person standing before the throne just simply points to Christ. While that settled the question of whether or not I was a Christian for a while, it never settled it finally. If I were honest, the fruit was not what I thought it should be and I knew that assurance of salvation, based on what I was seeing, just could not materialize. For me the struggle was real . . . and ongoing.

Since I was Reformed, I went to their confessions and catechism. That did not give me any relief. Instead, they made baptism a "sign" of the covenant and a "seal" of God's promises but never the promise itself. Reading Calvin certainly gave no solace either. In his *Institutes* he writes regarding faith and that the fruits of it can be false,

> *Experience shows that the reprobates are sometimes affected in a way so similar to the elect that even in their own judgment there is no difference between them. Hence,*

it is not strange, that by the Apostle a taste of heavenly gifts and by Christ himself a temporary faith is ascribed to them. Not that they truly perceive the power of spiritual grace and the sure light of faith; but the Lord, the better to convict them, and leave them without excuse, instills into their minds such a sense of goodness as can be felt without the Spirit of adoption . . . there is a great resemblance and affinity between the elect of God and those who are impressed for a time with a fading faith . . . Still it is correctly said, that the reprobate believe God to be propitious to them, inasmuch as they accept the gift of reconciliation, though confusedly and without due discernment; not that they are partakers of the same faith or regeneration with the children of God; but because, under a covering of hypocrisy they seem to have a principle of faith in common with them. Nor do I even deny that God illumines their mind to this extent . . . there is nothing inconsistent in this with the fact of his enlightening some with a present sense of grace, which afterwards proves evanescent.[3]

I tackled this on my blog when I wrote,

> A few years ago I took a course on Calvin's *Institutes.* However, I must have slept through this section because I honestly do not remember reading this. I think I would have been just as shocked that Calvin thought, and evidently taught, that one could have this elusive "confused faith" and that there are those who think they are among the elect and turn out to be among those chosen to damnation (Calvin's doctrine of double predestination).
>
> You: I think I'm saved . . . I think I'm saved . . . I think I'm saved.
>
> God: Nope. Just kidding.

Think about this: you are struggling to figure out if you are among God's elect. What are you to look to? Mostly the Calvinist/Reformed will tell you Christ Jesus but then quickly add that fruit is an evidence of your regeneration. The Heidelberg states that true faith has three parts: Knowledge, Assent and Trust. It also states

3. Calvin, *Institutes* 3.2.11.

> that those with "true faith" will do good works which is evidence of this true faith. However, Calvin writes that the reprobate (those chosen to damnation and not salvation) perceive the power of special grace, have the light of faith and that basically, "there is no difference between them. He goes on that they've tasted the Heavenly Gift but that Jesus has given them a "temporary faith". Okay, I need to stop here and make a comment: *How cruel can this be?*

This was downright cruel as it gave even what little bit of faith I had and was barely holding on to, along with the small deformed fruits I was exhibiting, nothing to stand upon with regard to assurance of salvation. I was sinking . . . fast.

You Only Think You are Saved

You are told to look at your fruit for the evidence that you have true faith, while at the same time, Calvin is teaching that your fruit proves nothing because you still may not have true faith.

Wait . . . What?!?

How am I to figure out if I'm among the elect? I may be doing the same good works as the reprobate. Or, I might just be a reprobate doing the same works, producing the same fruit of the Spirit, which the elect do. By this fruit, professing believers are supposed to be assured that they have true faith. Now, Calvinists, the Dutch Reformed, and Lutherans hold that true faith is a gift from God, but yet, the Reformed say the professing believer might just be fooled. Oh what dangerous ground we have stepped on. This is far worse than a slippery slope. This is not assurance. This is torment at its worst. If a person is struggling to believe that they are a true believer, look to their works, trust in Christ alone, acknowledge they are saved by grace alone, through faith alone, according to God's word alone; believing this, Calvin is saying they might still be a reprobate?

If this confused believer then goes to the pastor, he might say that they've seen fruit in their life and they are trusting Christ alone for salvation. Let me emphasize this point of Calvin's, "under a covering of hypocrisy, they seem to have a principle of faith in common."[4] They look saved, profess faith in Christ alone, it appears God has been propitious to them (meaning covered their sins in the righteousness of Christ) and yet they are not under God's protection? Besides this, "the reprobate never receives anything but a *confused awareness of grace* . . . [1]" So God has given them "confusion"? I thought God was not the author of confusion (cf. 1 Cor 14:33).

Joe Heschmeyer writes:

> Calvin sees this problem and proposes two equally unhelpful solutions:
>
> 1. "Meanwhile, believers are taught to examine themselves carefully and humbly, lest carnal security creep in and take the place of assurance of faith."
>
> 2. "Should it be objected, that believers have no stronger testimony to assure them of their adoption, I answer, that though there is a great resemblance and affinity between the elect of God and those who are impressed for a time with a fading faith, yet the elect alone have that full assurance which is extolled by Paul, and by which they are enabled to cry, Abba, Father."[5]

There is a serious problem here. Heschmeyer's chart, referenced in the above blog post, is correct to point out that the reprobate, under this "confused" grace, have all the evidences of true faith and yet are not actually saved. So the struggling believer cannot at all rely upon any evidence in their life to prove they have true faith? By even questioning salvation, is the believer actually showing they don't have salvation because they do not possess full assurance? This salvation becomes an illusion and none can ever have real or full assurance of salvation. Again, this is a cruel torment. This also means that God is promoting this illusion and by doing so, lying to the seemingly saved person by perpetuating the

4. Calvin, *Institutes* 3.2.11.

5. Heschmeyer, "Evanescent Grace."

idea that though they've been predestined to hell they're going to think they're saved on the way to hell.

So, how cruel is this? It is *absolutely* cruel. I cannot look to my faith or fruit because they just might be false. However, Calvin says that if I am fully assured of my salvation then I am saved. Problem is, I'm *not* fully assured, which is why I'm supposed to check my fruit; but the fruit can be false and by that the faith is false; and so I have no assurance, but if I have assurance, then I am saved. Circular reasoning anyone? This is a vicious cycle: you don't have full assurance and you are supposed to go to your fruit but the fruit is not really any good and since the fruit is bad you can't have assurance but you can have something that looks like true faith and good fruit and still not be truly saved. Round and round I went in my mind and heart, further down the spiraling drain of naval-gazing into near utter despair.

Heidelberg vs. Wittenberg

> The world is now full of sects who/which exclaim that Baptism is merely an external matter and that external matters are of no use. However, let it be ever so much an external matter; here stand God's Word and command which institute, establish, and confirm Baptism. However, whatever God institutes and commands cannot be useless but must be an altogether precious matter, even if it were worth less than a straw in appearance.[6]

In this next section I want to compare what the Heidelberg Catechism and in some places the Belgic Confession, along with the Lutheran Confessions (*Book of Concord*) say regarding the subject alongside the Scriptures. This is so that you, the reader, may see both what they say and what they don't as well as how they compare with the Scriptures. As you read through these passages, think about whether that sacrament which God has ordained actually does what He says it does or not. Do the Scriptures speak of God working through these ordinary means, in this case water,

6. Plass, *What Luther Says*, 43.

in connection to the Word itself and accomplishes what God tells us? *Or*, is it merely symbolic, or in the case of some Reformed, "presumptive regeneration"[7] regarding the promises of God?

KAT

I have written about the Reformed acronym KAT: Knowledge, Assent, and Trust. With each of these, the believer is asked a question:

- *K*-Knowledge

Do you have knowledge of the Gospel?

- *A*-Assent

Do you believe the message of the Scriptures?

- *T*-Trust

Do you trust entirely in Jesus Christ for your salvation?

Do you see how each of these is asking whether or not you are doing something? Each of these is relying upon you. However, I'm going to show how the Lutherans and, without meaning to sound redundant here, how the Scriptures view this. I will still use KAT.

- *K*-Knowledge

Know that Jesus died for the world.

- *A*-Assent

Assent that Jesus died for the world, for sinners, of which you are one simply because the Scriptures tell us.

- *T*-Trust

Trust that Jesus died for the world, because Scripture tells us this and you are among those for whom He died.

7. Cooper, *Great Divide*, 111. As Rev. Cooper notes, the most famous Reformed theologian who held to presumptive regeneration was Abraham Kuyper.

Can you see how this changes the perspective? It moves from something you have to do to what Jesus has done as told to us in the holy Scriptures. It is not about you, whether you're believing, assenting to, and trusting, rather it is about Jesus and His work of redemption for the world. You are part of that world. I am part of that world. No longer do I have to measure up to KAT to see if I have the proper knowledge, assenting to it and trusting. Instead, I'm looking to Jesus Christ who died for the world, who died for me (as a sinner in this fallen world) and who tells us He did this in God's word.

For Lutherans, baptism is the sacrament of invitation. "It is a washing that goes soul deep."[8] Baptism actually brings us into the Kingdom of God, clothed now with proper garments, made white as snow, having been sprinkled clean by the water with the Word. Since baptism is the work of God, He actually and effectually forgives, saves, and brings the one being baptized into both the visible (local) and invisible church of Christ. However, Calvinists, whether Presbyterian or Reformed, hold that this invitation is to join the visible church and one trusts the promises to someday be effectually done when faith is given, usually at a later date, when upon their confession of faith they are then mystically joined to the invisible church.

As I read more of what the Dutch Reformed believe regarding baptism, it begins to become clear that those "Lutheran undercurrents" I wrote of in an earlier chapter flow here as well. As my husband and I discussed this concept that baptism is simply a sign and seal, which has no actual soteriological (salvation) effect upon the one being baptism, he reminded me that we didn't really hold to the Reformed/Calvinistic view. Instead, as with other teachings in the Bible, we tried to hold to what it plainly said. Well, he did. Usually I was trying to figure God out and too often read into the verse or chapter what I was hearing from the Reformed camp. Therefore, some of what I will share as the Dutch Reformed, aka Heidelberg view, was not what either of us fully embraced. Once

8. Lehmann, *Lutheranism 101: Holy Baptism*, 13.

again, even on baptism we were told "You are too Lutheran in your view . . ."

Sacraments: Effective Means of Grace *or* Seals Confirming Grace?

Heidelberg View

So what does the Heidelberg Catechism teach? Why is it so different than the Lutheran view? It comes down to defining the term sacrament. The two views are very different. Lutherans view the sacraments as actually giving the person what it signifies while Calvinists/Reformed say it is a picture of that which it signifies. The choice is either receiving the actual promise of forgiveness or simply being given a picture of that promise.

In our home I have ample pictures of my husband and me when he proposed to me and of our wedding. However, the picture displays what happened but we are actually married. It is the difference between a two-dimensional photo of a memory and the reality that we are one in marriage. While looking at pictures can stir up the heart, it is the reality of us being husband and wife that truly matters. In the same way, if one looks at the elements of baptism as a reminder of promises but does not actually hold the reality that their sins were forgiven in the water with the Word, then it becomes like the picture of a wedding and loses the day-to-day reality of it.

The Reformed hold, as Brian Schwertley writes, that sacraments "are sensible signs, they are very effective in stimulating our souls and confirming our faith. With greater use of the senses they are effective in moving the heart."[9] However, for the Calvinist, they don't change the heart. For the Reformed, these are signs which point to something beyond themselves, whereas for Lutherans they are that something beyond, namely the actual promises of forgiveness.

9. Schwertley, *Sacraments*, 4.

The Heidelberg Catechism teaches, regarding sacraments, the following from Lord's Day 25,

> 66. Q. What are the sacraments?
> A. The sacraments are holy, visible signs and seals, appointed of God for this end, that by the use thereof He may the more fully declare and seal to us the promise of the gospel; namely, that He of grace grants us the remission of sins and life eternal, for the sake of the one sacrifice of Christ accomplished on the cross.
> 67. Q. Are, then, both the Word and the sacraments designed to direct our faith to the sacrifice of Jesus Christ on the cross as the only ground of salvation?
> A. Yes, indeed; for the Holy Spirit teaches us in the gospel and assures us by the sacraments that the whole of our salvation stands in the one sacrifice of Christ made for us on the cross.[10]

Notice that sacraments must have three things:

1. Holy
2. Visible
3. Appointed by God

In general, Christians who came out of the Reformation from Rome would agree with these requirements in order for them to be called sacraments. They are "holy" in the sense that the elements, for a time, are set apart for God's use. Indeed, water is visible, as are the bread and wine in the Lord's Supper. Third, they are things that Jesus told His church to do; baptize and participate in the body and blood of our Lord. It would be agreed that by the use of these sacraments, believers see the gospel visibly and that because the promises are seen assurance can grow. Where the difference comes is that baptism as a sign and seal only is where the Reformed end the power of a sacrament. As the Heidelberg states, these visible signs and seals are for visual benefit. They are reminders of what God promises but are not truly means of grace. Though the Reformed use the term "means of grace" which they

10. *Ecumenical and Reformed Creeds*, 47.

hold to be defined as "a medium, method, or instrument used to accomplish a certain purpose,"[11] they do not actually teach that baptism is the instrument used to accomplish the forgiveness of sins or regeneration.

For the Reformed, the Heidelberg continues in its explanation of what baptism does and what it does not do. The Heidelberg asks, "I, then, the outward washing with water itself the washing away of sin?" It answers in the negative. "No, for only the blood of Jesus Christ and the Holy Spirit cleanse us from all sins." Further it explains that it is to "assure us by this divine pledge and sign that we are spiritually cleansed . . ."[12] and utilizes the example of outwardly washing with an inward washing. However, it denies the efficacy of the sacrament because it denies what Scripture plainly says, "Baptism now saves . . ." (1 Pet 3:21).

The Reformed view of baptism is more of a covenantal perspective which marks out the individual as one who joins the visible community of believers but, in the case of infants and children, may not be actual believers yet. Many parents will hold to "presumptive regeneration" and only if they reject the gospel sometime in the future will they then say they were never regenerated to begin with. Theodore Beza, professor and pastor in Geneva (Calvin's successor there), who was the one to develop John Calvin's teachings on predestination and election while changing some aspects of Calvin's view on baptism even further, stated in the Colloquy of Montbâeliard in 1586 (a debate between Reformed and Lutheran men) the following:

> I answer: Infants sprinkled by water Baptism are *PROBABLY*, probably I say, considered sons of God. But we think that it is absurd to assert that they are renewed at that moment when they are baptized, such that they become new people with the old man destroyed. The reason for this is that children do not have faith, especially

11. Kampen, "Means of Grace."

12. *Ecumenical and Reformed Creeds*, 48.

> actual faith. But they are baptized in the faith of their parents.[13]

To Beza's statement that baptism is a sign but does not actually confer the grace it signified, Dr. Jakob Andreae, an author of the *Lutheran Formula of Concord* states emphatically,

> . . . the water of baptism has been ordained not for a representation, but for the delivery of a spiritual washing of regeneration in the name of the Trinity. The baptized are truly regenerated there . . . [14]

In answer to why infants should be baptized, the Heidelberg reveals what it truly believes about baptism. Infants are to be baptized in order to be "included in the covenant . . . as a sign of the covenant . . . engrafted into the Christian church and distinguished from children of unbelievers, as was done in the old covenant or testament by circumcision."[15] Once again, baptism is simply a sign that they are part of the Christian community (visible) with nothing having actually been done within them to make them a true part of the Christian church (invisible). As R.C. Sproul wrote, "The sacraments are a way to portray the gospel visibly and tangibly . . . though they are effective means of grace, they are effective in confirming our belief in Christ . . ."[16] The Heidelberg view lacks any efficacy to do that which the thing signifies. It is, as Luther would say, and I paraphrase, a sealed letter with nothing written therein.[17]

Further, the Reformed view holds that the sacraments deal more with sanctification than salvation. David R. Bickle writes that the *sacraments* do two things only: "1. *it* sustains faith in the gospel by confirming its promises . . . 2. *It* declares that the one who receives it is a true worshipper of God."[18] Utilizing the picture analogy the Reformed/Calvinist makes the sacraments shadows of

13. Andreae and Armstrong, *Lutheranism Vs. Calvinism*, 485.
14. Andreae and Armstrong, *Lutheranism Vs. Calvinism*, 519.
15. *Ecumenical and Reformed Creeds*, 48.
16. Sproul, "Focus of Sacraments."
17. Plass, *What Luther Says*, 54.
18. Bickle, "Seeing the Forgiveness of God."

the real. It is only a type or a picture of the reality and not what God uses (Means of Grace) to confer that reality to the person, namely the forgiveness of sins. Both baptism and the Lord's Supper are to be reminders, ever so powerful ones, of the gospel promises, yet they do not actually confer those promises. Bickle writes that Calvin believed that baptism in particular only confirmed that Jesus washed away the sins of the church: "an outward sign by which the Lord seals on our consciences the promises of his good will toward us in order to sustain the weakness of our faith; and we in turn attest our piety toward him in the presence of the Lord and of his angels and before men."[19]

Here, Calvin makes the sacraments something we do for God, it will "attest our piety toward him . . ." rather than a work which God does for us, forgive, renew, strengthens and sustains. Elsewhere Calvin writes that the grace of God "is by no means so annexed to them (sacraments) that whoso receives the sign also gains possession of the thing . . . for the signs are administered alike to reprobate and elect, but the reality reaches the latter only."[20]

When one reads the Heidelberg, specifically Lord's Day (LD) 26, if you do not continue to Lord's Day 27, you may walk away thinking that the framers of this catechism believed baptism actually conferred that which it signified, namely the forgiveness of sins. However, continue reading and it states,

> 72. Q. Is, then, the outward washing with water itself the washing away of sin?
> A. No, for only the blood of Jesus Christ and the Holy Spirit cleanse us from all sins.[21]

So while in Lord's Day 26 one gets the impression that the Dutch Reformed were also Lutheran in their view on the effect of baptism, they actually are not. The answer to Question 73, "Why, then, does the Holy Spirit call baptism the 'washing of regeneration' and 'the washing away of sins'"? The writers respond that the

19. Bickle, "Seeing the Forgiveness of God."

20. Beveridge, "Mutual Consent," 217.

21. *Ecumenical and Reformed Creeds*, 47.

Bible is giving us only similarity. God using the substance of water compares baptism's effects to that of water washing away dirt but it does not actually wash away sins. The Reformed, whether Swiss, Dutch, or Presbyterian hold to the idea that, as Beza says, baptism,

> . . . is only a signification and representation of a spiritual washing, in which the soul is washed, that is, is cleaned from sins, which happens through the blood of Christ. The external and elemental water of baptism signifies and represents this washing. But it is not itself a washing or bath, nor can it deliver or accomplish this.[22]

The Reformed, as much as they may insist on an infant being baptized, believe that baptism in water is to be understood figuratively and metaphorically as it only "signifies the spiritual washing that is inward."[23] The water signifies the blood of Christ and the outward washing is a picture of an inward washing that may take place later in life through faith. They will argue that they do not make baptism a "bare sign"[24] yet they do not hold that, as Scripture states, "Baptism now saves you" (1 Pet 3:21). This is because of their view on the teaching of election and how those with true faith can never fall away. The Reformed view of baptism, in some circles, is that for the elect it may or may not at the time the water is applied actually regenerate the child or adult. It is a sign to others of the promise God makes in salvation but it is not salvific. Other variations of Reformed or Presbyterians may hold in presumptive regeneration at the time of baptism but one must still have a baptism with the Spirit in order to be regenerated. When I thought through this, I began to realize the Reformed, Presbyterian, Calvinist views hold to two baptisms: one with water, the other of the Spirit, whereas Scripture speaks of one baptism when it says, "One Lord, one faith, one baptism" (Eph 4:5).

22. Andreae and Armstrong, *Lutheranism Vs. Calvinism*, 519.

23. "What does an outward and invisible sign of an inward spiritual grace mean?" https://www.answers.com/Q/What_does_an_outward_and_invisible_sign_of_an_inward_spiritual_grace_mean.

24. *Ecumenical and Reformed Creeds*, 47.

Furthermore, by removing the grace that is actually conferred in the water and the Word, the Reformed establish that they are simply signs which signify a work of God and merely represent that which they picture for us. The Reformed say that the sacraments are means of grace, that which God uses the ordinary to give the extraordinary. In other words, God uses ordinary substances, bread, wine, and water, to affect grace in the person receiving it. However, as I dug deeper into their teachings it became apparent that what these elements signified did not actually confer grace but simply were a picture of that grace from which believers were to be an encouragement to faith. Baptism without the Spirit actually doing what it signifies, that is, regenerating the sinner, becomes an empty sign even if it still pictures the work of Christ. It becomes a simple picture and not the real thing. It is an empty and vacuous practice and no longer a sacrament in its true meaning of the term.

Reverting Back to Types and Shadows

When I began to think about baptism as merely a sign signifying the truth but not actually conferring that which it pictured, my mind went to the Old Testament's use of types and shadows. In the Old Testament we have sacrifices of animals to propitiate for the sins of the people. Hebrews reminds us that these did not actually forgive sins but that they were pictures of that final and ultimate sacrifice of Jesus Christ, whom God had prepared a body for, to suffer and die and actually forgive sins. Mulling this Reformed teaching (signs and seals) over in my mind, I thought that what was happening was that the Reformed were making baptism (and the Lord's Supper) a sign and seal but not the reality. Then, as I was reading the Colloquy of Montbâeliard I came across Dr. Andreae saying the same thing:

> The rite of immersion or sprinkling of water in Baptism is not representative only. And even though the rite of immersion or sprinkling in baptism is a certain representation of spiritual mortification and regeneration, it nevertheless was not instituted for the sake of representing,

> but rather of accomplishing regeneration, let we seek out and trust in shadows and figures rather than body and truth.[25]

Two Baptisms

For the Reformed and many evangelicals there are two baptisms. The Reformed would place water baptism as first and then the spiritual baptism as a later event in the life of a child brought into the covenant community through the waters. The evangelical places the spiritual baptism as first. One must first accept Jesus and be born again of the Spirit and then they choose to be baptized in water to express what has already occurred in their spirit earlier. Therefore, both of these groups have two baptisms, each done at separate times and by separate entities: water by man and spiritual by God. This goes against the plain reading of the Scriptures which states there is "One Lord, one faith and *one baptism*" (Eph 4:5). The Nicene Creed affirmed this when it says that "we confess *one baptism* for the forgiveness of sins."

Therefore, in the Reformed view we find that the sacraments are not fully a means of grace for they do not affect what they signify immediately but only probably and that at a later date and time. Second, since they make the sacraments only signs and seals, this means they are empty of the power of grace which God has deigned them to confer. This results in reverting back to the types and shadows of the Old Testament but lacking the reality which God says they actually have. Finally, we conclude that both evangelicals and Reformed disobey Scripture in creating two baptisms rather than the one which God's word testifies to.

Lutheran View

In light of a summary of the Reformed view from the Heidelberg Catechism and those of Calvinistic background, we should look

25. Andreae and Armstrong, *Lutheranism Vs. Calvinism*, 519.

at what the Lutheran view is. I know many Reformed who respect and admire Martin Luther but disagree with his view on baptism. Often the charge is that Luther did not go far enough in reforming and that is where Calvin and Beza picked up the gauntlet. However, the more I study the more I realize that Luther did not reform the church in Germany on his own. Princes, pastors, and doctors of theology worked with him to bring the comfort of the true gospel to their people. It is through their writings that I will share with you the specifically Lutheran approach to the sacraments.

First, we need to understand what a sacrament is. When we came out of evangelicalism we did not understand this word so that is why I include a short explanation here. A sacrament is a combination of two terms: *sacra* meaning "mystery" literally "something sacred . . ." or "holy" and *meant* meaning "thing it means." The glossary in *Concordia: The Lutheran Confessions* defines it as "A Sacrament is a sacred act instituted by God in which God Himself has joined His Word of promise to a visible element, and by which He offers, gives, and seals the forgiveness of sins earned by Christ."[26]

What are means of grace? They are the avenue, the way that God confers that which he promises in water: forgiveness of sins, new life, regeneration, justification, and all the gospel promises which flow from Christ. The Large Catechism in *Concordia: The Lutheran Confessions* states, baptism

> . . . is no longer mere water . . . but water comprehended in God's Word and command and sanctified by them (Eph 5:26–27) . . . a divine, heavenly, holy and blessed water, and whatever other terms we can find to praise it. This is all because of the Word, which is a heavenly, holy Word, which no one can praise enough. For it has, and is able to do, all that God is and can do (Is. 55:10–11).[27]

In the Augsburg Apology, we read that "these rites (sacraments) have God's command and the promise of grace."[28] These

26. Dau, *Concordia*, 673.

27. Dau, *Concordia*, 425.

28. Dau, *Concordia*, 184.

are the means by which God gives faith (true saving faith). Since saving faith is a gift, one receives this faith through the water connected with the Word. It is not the water, though that is the means, but it is God who connects baptism with forgiveness and salvation. The churches of Lutheranism teach what the Augsburg Confession states, "Concerning baptism, our churches teach that baptism is necessary for salvation and that God's grace is offered through baptism . . ." (AC IX). "Baptism is not purely a symbol of grace that is received through faith. Baptism genuinely offers and gives grace to the recipient."[29] Rather than being a sign and seal only of the promise, these gifts actually confer the grace they depict. Lutherans do not hold that the water has some special quality but it is the One who ordained the waters of baptism who saves. Unlike the Reformed, Lutherans hold that baptism actually saves because Peter says that "baptism now saves you" (1 Pet 3:21).

The three parts of a sacrament for Lutherans are

1. Commanded by God
2. Visible elements
3. Offers God's grace (forgiveness)

Luther held that sacraments had this third part because Scripture taught it. When Jesus said, regarding the wine at the Last Supper, this is my blood for the forgiveness of your sins, he wasn't using cryptic imagery but was telling his disciples that when they participated in the Supper the wine is His blood and offers the recipient actual forgiveness of sins. In the waters of baptism, the apostles' first call was to "repent *and* be baptized for the forgiveness of sins" (Acts 2:38–39, emphasis added). God gives true faith in and with the waters of baptism; it is the gift of the Spirit that Peter speaks of in his first sermon on Pentecost. Since God grants that faith, baptism is not a letter sealed "without any writing in it"[30] but has written into it the actual conferring of the forgiveness of sins.

29. Cooper, *Great Divide*, 110.

30. Plass, *What Luther Says*, 54.

Through the means of grace "God creates faith in Christ Jesus" and baptism, which is the means through which God washes us, gives us that gift of the Spirit, true faith. Baptism, according to the Scriptures, is one of the instruments of salvation. Whether through the Word preached or the water with the Word, God brings forgiveness of sins to sinners, granting them true faith through these means. It is why, in Lutheranism, Word and sacrament are those instruments which help us both enter the Christian life and make progress in expressing that faith. Both the Word and sacrament are how God brings His promises of forgiveness, regeneration, true faith, and salvation to sinners. God uses ordinary means (instruments) to confer the extraordinary, the Holy Spirit Himself. In the explanation of *Luther's Small Catechism* we read, "Because they (sacraments) are established by God's command and convey His grace, we distinguish the sacraments from ceremonies and rites established by human beings."[31] As you can see, the Lutheran view of baptism is that it actually conveys to the sinner that which it signifies. It is no bare sign, nor is it a covenantal promise which may or may not actually happen at a later date. When Scripture says "Baptism now saves . . ." it is an immediate act of God not a promise of a later work of grace. In other words, as the explanation writes, the sacraments are "God's Word doing what it says and actually giving and delivering to us what it promises."[32]

Luther wrote in his *Small Catechism* this on baptism:

> What is Baptism?
>
> Baptism is not just plain water, but it is the water included in God's command and combined with God's Word.
>
> Which is that Word of God?
>
> Christ our Lord says in the last chapter of Matthew:
>
> "Therefore go and make disciples of all nations, baptizing them in the name of the Father and of the Son and of the Holy Spirit.[33]

31. Luther, *Luther's Small Catechism*, 282.
32. Luther, *Luther's Small Catechism*, 281.
33. Luther, *Luther's Small Catechism*, 285.

That is a simple way to understand baptism. It is from God, commanded by Jesus Christ and instituted for the life of the church. It is not plain water but water with the Word which makes baptism what it is: a means of grace. God grants saving faith, the gift of the Holy Spirit spoken of in Acts 2:38–39, which says, "Repent and be baptized every one of you in the name of Jesus Christ for the forgiveness of your sins, and you will receive the gift of the Holy Spirit . . ."

Gifted Faith for Infants and Adults

Whether an adult or an infant, faith is a gift given by God and not automatically dwelling within them. We do not, as the Arminians and evangelicals teach, all have faith which we must exercise to believe in Jesus Christ and by that decision become Christians. Rather, that saving faith is a gift of God granted to us through Word and sacrament. Faith is not an intellectual ability to believe. Scripture reminds us that faith is a gift given by God to sinners who are spiritually dead. God delivers the gift of salvation through the water and the Word. Indeed, Luther calls baptism a "precious thing" when he writes in his Large Catechism,

> . . . we value Baptism as an excellent, glorious, and exalted. We contend and fight for Baptism chiefly because the world is now so full of sects arguing that Baptism is an outward thing and that outward things are of no benefit. But let Baptism be a thoroughly outward thing. Here stand God's Word and command, which institute, establish, and confirm Baptism. What God institutes and commands cannot be an empty thing. It must be a most precious thing, even though it looked like it had less value than a straw.[34]

Salvation by grace through faith is a prominent teaching in the Bible. Paul writes to the Roman and Ephesian churches the following:

34. Luther quoted in Dau, *Concordia*, 424.

> . . . and are justified by his grace as a gift, through the redemption that is in Christ Jesus. (Rom 3:24)

> *Therefore, since we have been justified by faith, we have peace with God through our Lord Jesus Christ. Through him we have also obtained access by faith into this grace in which we stand, and we rejoice in hope of the glory of God.* Rom 5:1–2

> For *by grace you have been saved through faith. And this is not your own doing; it is the gift of God, not a result of works, so that no one may boast.* (Eph 2:8–9)

Saving faith is not something that we inherently possess but must be given by God Himself. How does God give us, confer to sinners, this faith? Through baptism. Christ said, "Whoever believes and is baptized will be saved" (Mark 16:16). Peter, by inspiration of the Holy Spirit says to us that "Baptism saves . . ." As the *Larger Catechism* says, "the power, work, profit, fruit, and purpose of Baptism is this—to save." Truly we can say, with Martin Luther, that baptism is an "unspeakable treasure" for it does exactly what it signifies; it saves.

However, baptism doesn't stop there. One thing I have learned over the past two years is that baptism continues its work in us. Martin Luther said that when we wash our face it should remind us of our baptism. When Satan, the world, and our own sinful flesh rail against us, we are to remember "I am baptized." In fact, Luther writes,

> So when our sins and conscience oppress us, we strengthen ourselves and take comfort and say, 'Nevertheless, I am baptized. And if I am baptized, it is promised to me that I shall be saved and have eternal life, both in soul and body.[35]

Baptism both promises and brings with it "victory over death and the devil, forgiveness of sin, God's grace, the entire Christ and the Holy Spirit with His gifts."[36] Truly it is an "unspeakable trea-

35. Luther quoted in Dau, *Concordia*, 427.

36. Luther quoted in Dau, *Concordia*, 426.

sure" upon which we may rest because it is not my work, or your work of faith, but rather, it is God's gift given to all freely. Baptism is a work which is not a "one and done" in the past event. Rather, it is the work of God which continues through our life. When the enemy attacks us or our conscience becomes bowed under the load of sin, we are to remind ourselves that "I *am* baptized" in the here and now. We should not say, "I was baptized" as if it were something we did to tell others of our faith, rather in a continual mode of "I am baptized."

When I struggled for assurance, the Reformed confessions and catechisms pointed me to the fruit produced in my life. However, the fruit we produce here in this sinful, sad, and fallen world will never be perfect and God requires perfection. Then, when I could not look at the fruit in my life, I was told that the Holy Spirit would assure me that I was truly His. However, struggling with assurance meant that I was also not getting that assurance from the Holy Spirit that I belonged to Christ. Where could I look? The Devil was taunting me with accusations and torturing me with doubts. The world told me I wasn't a "good Christian" after all, and to look at all my faults and hypocritical behavior. My own flesh condemned me because I know my sins most personally.

In the Colloquy, which I've referred to earlier, Beza says that our assurance of salvation does not come through the outward sign of baptism but rather "should be sought from the effects of the Holy Spirit, namely when we feel such movements of the Holy Spirit in us that bear witness that we have been truly regenerated and adopted and are sons of God."[37] My own question was this: How, if I doubt, can I possibly feel the Spirit, whose work I doubt?

Dr. Andreae responds beautifully with great comfort when he says,

> How therefore is such a conscience able to be cheered? If he should in fact be left to the internal moving of the Holy Spirit, which he does not feel, but rather the contrary, desperation will increase, not diminish. It is necessary therefore to run to the Word and the Sacraments

37. Andreae, and Armstrong. *Lutheranism Vs. Calvinism*, 530–31.

> and they should be made us of more than those ruminations that cause despair.[38]

Here was true comfort. I no longer was to look inward for assurance. I was not to look at my faith, my response, my love, my lack of any of these things either, but look to Christ and His work of salvation in the water and the Word of baptism. There comfort is truly found. It no longer rests on my feeble acts or feelings but on the mighty power of an Almighty God in the sacraments.

> Sin, disturb my soul no longer: *I am baptized into Christ*!
> I have comfort even stronger: Jesus' cleansing sacrifice.
> Should a guilty conscience seize me, since my baptism did release me
> In a dear forgiving flood, sprinkling me with Jesus' blood?
> ("God's Own Child," verse 2)[39]

One Lord, One Faith, One Baptism

Lutherans, and the Bible, hold to one baptism and not two (see above regarding the Reformed and evangelical position of two distinct baptisms). There is one singular baptism which is outer and confers the inner at that moment. There is no waiting for a later date for the promises to become effective. Rather, baptism consists of water and the Spirit. Jesus said, "Unless someone is born again of water and the spirit, he cannot enter the kingdom of heaven" (John 3:5). Growing up evangelical, we were taught that being "born of water" referred to natural birth. However, when reforming in doctrine and practice I then wondered how that can be because not all children are fully birthed; many die in the womb. What then, happens to them? Thinking about this critically, it soon dawned on me that this interpretation could not be. There must, then, be another interpretation of this.

Dr. Andreae states, "Water without the Spirit is not a Baptism, nor is spirit a Baptism without water, but water with the spirit

38. Andreae and Armstrong, *Lutheranism Vs. Calvinism*, 556–57.

39. Lutheran Church Missouri Synod, *Lutheran Service Book*, 594.

and spirit with the water joined together with Christ's word, under which word is the Holy Spirit."[40] Here, Jesus joined both water and the spirit so that one would be born again, regenerated. Luther reiterated this when he wrote in the small catechism, "Baptism . . . is a gracious water of life and a washing of regeneration in the Holy Spirit."[41]

Luther wrote in the Large Catechism,

> How can water do such great things?
> Answer: It is not the water indeed that does them, but the word of God which is in and with the water, and faith, which trusts such word of God in the water. For without the word of God the water is simple water and no baptism. But with the word of God it is a baptism . . . [42]

The Scriptures speak of baptism and the Spirit together often. The external element of water joined with the Word is what makes baptism a sacrament and a means of grace. When Jesus said one must be born of water and the Spirit he was not speaking physical birth and then spiritual birth, but had joined the water with the Word in the work of the Spirit to confer the grace of forgiveness of sins and life eternal. When the Word is joined to the Spirit through the Word of God and one is baptized in the name of the Father, Son, and Holy Spirit, then one is truly washed from sins, regenerated, renewed, and becomes a new creation in Christ Jesus.

Baptism, therefore, is not a metaphor nor is it a sign and seal without anything written therein (the empty letter Luther spoke of). Nor is baptism a sign which holds the place of the promises until the person responds in faith to those promises signified but not actually conferred in the waters of baptism. As Dr. Andreae says,

> it (baptism) is, is, is a washing of regeneration.[43] (Love his emphasis on "is")

40. Andreae and Armstrong, *Lutheranism Vs. Calvinism*, 522–23.

41. Dau, *Concordia*, 340.

42. Dau, *Concordia*, 425.

43. Andreae and Armstrong, *Lutheranism Vs. Calvinism*, 520.

In Lutheranism, there is no distinguishing between the two. Instead that which is signified in the washing of baptism is a reality and is "actually a washing of the water of regeneration."[44]

Brace for Mind-Blowing Comfort in Baptismal Waters

> "Let your baptism be your armor; your faith, your helmet; your love, your spear; your patient endurance, your panoply."—Ignatius of Antioch, AD 110

Have you ever read a verse that you have read previously over a dozen times and then it suddenly hit you as if you'd never read it before? That is exactly what happened to me once at the ladies Bible study.

> I will sprinkle clean water on you, and you shall be clean from all your uncleannesses, and from all your idols I will cleanse you. And, I will give you a new heart, and a new spirit I will put within you. And I will remove the heart of stone from your flesh and give you a heart of flesh. And I will put My Spirit within you, and cause you to walk in My statutes and be careful to obey My rules. (Ezek 36:25–27)

These verses hit me like a ton of bricks . . . wait, no, it didn't land on me harsh and bury me. Let me rephrase this: These verses broke all over me like water on parched ground. There was nothing I could do but let it soak into me, refreshing me, filling me with joy, and showering me with God's love. Read it again, my friends. If you grew up Baptist or even Covenantal Baptist, read it and recognize the order of things in it. Here, let me list it:

First, it is God's work, for He says, "I will." Second, what does He do? "Sprinkle with clean water . . ." Water. Don't spiritualize it and try to say this is a figure of speech and water means "Spirit" because in the text Ezekiel then says specifically "Spirit" later on. So, He sprinkles clean water on you, on me. Third, notice the result of the water being sprinkled on you; you will be clean. Clean! Washed

44. Andreae and Armstrong, *Lutheranism Vs. Calvinism*, 519.

. . . from *all* your uncleanness. You are washed clean from all your sins! Hallelujah! There, right there, is where assurance began to flood my soul. I had never seen this proper order before.

All my life, baptism was what you did *after* you were born-again, or made a decision, or gave your heart to Jesus. It was *never* before. Baptism was something you did to tell the world you were a believer and to commit to Jesus. Ezekiel says the opposite. Somehow we all got it backwards (except for the Lutherans). Baptist, Calvinist, Reformed, Presbyterian, they all put the change of the heart before the cleansing by the water through the Word. They all made the water something other than water so that it fit, like a square peg into a round hole, their own theological viewpoint. Instead of letting the Scriptures speak plainly, they flipped it and with that flipping, removed true assurance of salvation and opened the door for all kinds of error.

Fourth, what is it that actually happens when the water with the Word is sprinkled upon us? Ezekiel tells us: "I will give you a new heart, and a new spirit I will put within you . . ." We are given a new heart.

So that my evangelicals understand this, it is akin to what John said in his Gospel that we are "born again" or regenerated. Prior to the work of God's grace we are dead in sin, with a stony heart. When God sprinkles us with clean water He gives us that new birth and a new heart of flesh. He also gives us His Spirit who works within us to live for Him. The Holy Spirit is the one who causes us to walk in the ways of the Lord and actually want to obey his commands. This is all given via the waters of baptism with the Word.

The order in this verse is crucial to understanding what happens in baptism. This is also testified to by Peter when he correlates the flood of Noah with the waters of baptism. He writes that baptism now saves just as the ark saved the eight in Genesis.

> Baptism, which corresponds to this, now saves you, not as a removal of dirt from the body but as an appeal to God for a good conscience, through the resurrection of Jesus Christ, who has gone into heaven and is at the right

> hand of God, with angels, authorities, and powers having been subject to him." For if we have been united with him in a death like his, we shall certainly be united with him in a resurrection like his. (1 Pet 3:21–22)

There have been several texts, which when read plainly, have shown the connection between water baptism and regeneration, salvation, forgiveness of sins. One such Scripture is:

> And Peter said to them, "Repent and be baptized every one of you in the name of Jesus Christ for the forgiveness of your sins, and you will receive the gift o the Holy Spirit. For the promise is for you and for your children and for all who are far off, everyone whom the Lord our God calls to himself." (Acts 2:38–39)

Please notice the connection between repent and baptism. It says, Repent *and* be baptized . . . Odd when a verse you've read all your life suddenly becomes plain and clearly says something different than what you were taught. Honestly, this verse was always taught as: Repent first, *then* be baptized later. But this is not what the text says. It joins repentance and baptism together, for it says and, not, then. What came as a greater shock was what repentance and baptism do or result in actually forgiveness. Read it again: Repent *and* be baptized . . . for the forgiveness of your sins . . . Did you catch it? We repent and are baptized and receive the forgiveness of sins, the gift of the Holy Spirit. An adult believer is being told to repent *and* be baptized for forgiveness. One has to ask again, how did I miss this?

Chris Rosebrough of Pirate Christian has a handout on how the earliest Christians understood this text and he quote Barnabas's writing on this text,

> Regarding baptism, we have the evidence of Scripture that Israel would refuse to accept the washing which confers the remission of sins . . . Observe there how he describes both the water and the cross in the same figure. His meaning is, 'Blessed are those who go down into the water with their hopes set on the cross.' Here he is saying that after we have stepped down into the water, burdened

> with sin and defilement, we come up out of it bearing fruit, with reverence in our hearts and the hope of Jesus in our souls . . . [45]

Further, he quotes Hermas, "there is no other repentance except that which took place when we went down into the water and obtained the remission of our former sins" (The Shepherd 4:3:1–2, AD 80.

Please notice how close these quotes are in dating to that of the writings of the New Testament and the lives of the apostles themselves. If these understandings of baptism and the interpretations of the texts were wrong, wouldn't the apostles—still alive—namely John, have corrected them in letters? However, we have no corrections and the apostles of Jesus were certainly not reticent to publically rebuke false teachers in their day.

There is yet another item which kept rolling around in my mind: Hebrews states Jesus is the "greater" of all things, angels (Heb 1:4, 6, 8) prophets (Heb 3:3–4; 4:8–9) and priests (Heb 7:26–28), etc. If, then, John the Baptist's baptism was for the forgiveness of sins, then why, under evangelicalism, were we taught Jesus' baptism does not forgive sins but is rather our testimony or, as Presbyterian and Reformed churches would say, a sign and seal of the promises of God but not actually the promises? Would not the baptism of Jesus either be better than John's or at the least accomplish what John's baptism did? The Gospel of Mark records:

> John appeared, baptizing in the wilderness and proclaiming a baptism of repentance *for the forgiveness of sins.* (Mark 1:4, emphasis added)

John is perplexed as to why Jesus is coming to be baptized because in those waters sins are forgiven. For years I wondered about why John questioned Jesus' coming to him. Now, reading the Scriptures simply, with no theological gymnastics involved, it is because baptism is for the forgiveness of sins and Jesus did not need to be forgiven. The Scriptures do not say that people repented

45. Letter of Barnabus 11:1–10 (AD 74) quoted in Rosebrough, "What the Bible Teaches."

and then were baptized. No, it says that the baptism itself was one of repentance for the forgiveness of sins.

> Just as the Father and Holy Spirit were present at Jesus' baptism so now, as Luther says, "He Himself is there through His kindness and His love for men, because He desires to dwell in me. It is not an empty toke; but the power of the Father, the Son and the Holy Ghost is there and does not merely mark me externally before men but make a different person of me before God so that just as a person is born of a woman in sin, so he is born of Baptism to righteousness and life eternal.[46]

Reading the Scriptures for what they actually say, one begins to understand why Lutheranism stands out amongst other denominations. I have heard often at church and in Bible studies that "Is means is." It is a way to summarize that as Lutherans we simply take the Word to say what it means and mean what it says. In the *Small Catechism*, Luther writes on the benefits of baptism: "It works forgiveness of sins, rescues from death and the devil, and gives eternal salvation to all who believe this, as the words and promises of God declare."[47]

If, then, John the Baptist's baptism worked repentance for the forgiveness of sins, and he is the lesser and Jesus the greater, how can one say Jesus' baptism, in the name of the blessed Triune God, does nothing. From evangelical to Reformed, baptism is either just an act of obedience the believer does to announce to the world, or at least those in attendance, that they've joined the church or it is merely an outward sign of a possible inward work of grace. Yet, Scripture has said that baptism actually gives to the person, infant or adult, that which it signifies: forgiveness of sins. John Theodore Mueller, in his theological work wrote, "Baptism bestows nothing else than what the Gospel offers and imparts; it works forgiveness of sins."[48] He goes on to list the verses which teach this:

46. Plass, *What Luther Says*, 46.
47. Luther, *Luther's Small Catechism*, 23.
48. Mueller, *Christian Dogmatics*, 492.

- Acts 2:38: washes away sin
- Acts 22:16: sanctifies and cleanses
- Ephesians 5:26: regenerates and saves
- Titus 3:5: washing of regeneration
- 1 Peter 3:21: baptism . . . now saves you (comparing Noah's flood with the waters of baptism)

Dr. Mueller continues that what "the Holy Spirit does through the Gospel, working and strengthening faith (Rom 1:16, 1 Cor 2:4) this he does also through Baptism (see 1 Peter and Titus 3)." Luther wrote, "By the Word such power is imparted to Baptism that it is a laver of regeneration."[49]

Laver of Regeneration

The laver was used in the Old Testament where priests needed to wash with water before entering the tabernacle and later the temple to serve the Lord. Luther is not the first to use this term as we consider the following quotes:

> For since you have read, O Trypho, as you yourself admitted, the doctrines taught by our Savior, I do not think that I have done foolishly in adding some short utterances of His to the prophetic statements. *Wash therefore, and be now clean, and put away iniquity from your souls, as God bids you be washed in this laver, and be circumcised with the true circumcision* . . . The command of circumcision, again, bidding [them] always circumcise the children on the eighth day, was a type of the true circumcision, by which we are circumcised from deceit and iniquity through Him who rose from the dead on the first day after the Sabbath, [namely through] our Lord Jesus Christ.[50]

49. Luther, *Triglot*, 739 quoted in Mueller, *Christian Dogmatics*, 492.

50. *Dialogue with Trypho* by Justin (AD 160) quoted in Rosebrough, "What the Bible Teaches" (emphasis added).

St. Paul writes to the Colossian Christians:

> In him also you were circumcised with a circumcision made without hands, by putting off the body of the flesh, by *the circumcision of Christ*, having been *buried with him in baptism*, in which you were also raised with him through faith in the powerful working of God, who raised him from the dead. (Col 2:11–12)

Paul connects baptism to circumcision. While I was Dutch Reformed the teaching was that this was a sign and seal of the promises of God just as circumcision was. However, if we follow the pattern of Scripture that the works of God in Christ go from lesser to greater, then this circumcision which is now baptism actually is done by God when He buried us in baptism into Christ.

> Who is the one who is born of the Spirit and is made Spirit? It is one who is renewed in the Spirit of his mind. It is one who is regenerated by water and the Holy Spirit. We *receive the hope of eternal life through the laver of regeneration* and renewing of the Holy Spirit. And elsewhere the apostle Peter says: "You shall be baptized with the Holy Spirit." For who is he that is baptized with the Holy Spirit but he who is born again through water and the Holy Spirit? Therefore the Lord said of the Holy Spirit, "Truly, truly, I say to you, except a man be born again by water and the Spirit, he cannot enter into the kingdom of God." And therefore he declared that we are born of him into the kingdom of God by being born again by water and the Spirit.[51]

> While I was lying in darkness . . . I thought it indeed difficult and hard to believe . . . that divine mercy was promised for my salvation, *so that anyone might be born again and quickened unto a new life by the laver of the saving water*, he might put off what he had been before, and, although the structure of the body remained, he might change himself in soul and mind. . . . But afterwards, when the stain of my past life had been washed

51. Ambrose of Milan, *Of the Holy Spirit* 3.10.64 (AD 381), quoted in Rosebrough, "What the Bible Teaches" (emphasis added).

> away by means of the water of rebirth, a light from above poured itself upon my chastened and now pure heart; afterwards, through the Spirit which is breathed from heaven, a second birth made of me a new man.[52]

> And the bishop shall lay his hand upon them [the newly baptized], invoking and saying: 'O Lord God, who did count these worthy of deserving the *forgiveness of sins by the laver of regeneration,* make them worthy to be filled with your Holy Spirit and send upon them thy grace [in confirmation], that they may serve you according to your will.[53]

Each of these Christian men write that it is in the waters that one is given new life, forgiveness of sins, and eternal life. They write nothing new, nor have they created some doctrine and teaching which does not come directly out of the Bible. In the broad evangelicalism we see in the world the value, gifts of grace, and reality of baptism have been removed. The early church did no such thing but understood that when Scripture said "Baptism now saves," it meant that forgiveness, regeneration, justification, and salvation was actually conferred by the water and the Word in baptism.

This reductionist view by the evangelicals and their predecessors the Anabaptists have removed all those gifts. Zwingli (a reformer from the Swiss churches) denied the efficacy of baptism because he refused to believe that the promises God gives in His Word have been joined to the sacrament. A sacrament is the means of giving the person that which is promised through ordinary elements. Augustine said that when the Word is joined to the ordinary, water, bread, and wine, it becomes a sacrament. The evangelical, however, looks at the waters of baptism as just water. The Lutheran view has maintained that God does not just promise with signs and seals (a Reformed/Presbyterian view) but accomplishes those promises.

52. Cyprian of Carthage, *To Donatus* 3–4 (AD 246), quoted in Rosebrough, "What the Bible Teaches" (emphasis added).

53. Hippolytus, *The Apostolic Tradition* 22:1 (AD 215), quoted in Rosebrough, "What the Bible Teaches" (emphasis added).

While the Reformed will baptize their children and infants, they deny that baptism is a means of regeneration and that it is the means through which Christ joins that person (adult or infant) to His spiritual body. Instead, baptism is akin to circumcision and merely marks out the child as a member of the outer church. For the Reformed these things are merely symbolic and do not actually confer to the individual the gifts of God's grace. Zwingli said, "Water cannot do such great things; it is the Spirit who must accomplish them."[54] However, as pointed out in the Scriptures previously written here, the Scriptures actually do tell us that baptism regenerates, forgives us of our sins, and saves.

Down that slippery slope of baptism simply being a sign and seal, as Luther said, "A sealed letter with nothing written therein . . . . come to the evangelical view."[55] Here, baptism is no longer a work of God but an act of obedience after one is born again. Truly, baptism is the initiation rite of the believer; however, perspective makes all the difference. Either baptism is the work of God or a work of men and women. Either baptism is a gift to God's people whereby He forgives, regenerates, and saves or it is just an empty symbol. If an empty symbol, then one does not need to be baptized. "Why?" One may say, "I attend church, Bible study, worship. Why do I need to be baptized? Everyone knows I'm a Christian." From an empty symbol (Reformed view) one easily slides into an unnecessary tradition that does nothing for the believer, adult or child.

Scripture Speaks

In this chapter I have already gone through the Dutch Reformed view (Reformed) and the Lutheran view, and given some quotes from the early church and how they viewed baptism. Interspersed were Scriptures which spoke of water baptism and its link to

54. Mueller, *Christian Dogmatics*, 494.

55. Dau, *Concordia*, 426.

regeneration. In this section I will simply review more verses from God's Word.

First, let us review Acts 2:38–39, once again reading it plainly: "And Peter said to them, 'Repent and be baptized every one of you in the name of Jesus for the forgiveness of your sins, and you will receive the gift of the Holy Spirit."

What has stood out to me as the Scriptures are read plainly, without presuppositions (which granted is very hard to do on any subject), it becomes clear that Peter's instructions were to repent *and* be baptized *for* the forgiveness of sins. Peter did not say to repent for the forgiveness of sins alone. No, he added be baptized for the forgiveness of sins to the call to repent. Peter links repentance and baptism as bringing about the forgiveness of sins. Therefore, according to Scripture, baptism is not something done afterwards as a ceremony or a witness to others that you have repented. As Luther wrote, "There is here no work done by us, but a treasure which He gives us."[56] Instead, it is revealed to be a true means of grace. Through baptism God offers and conveys to sinners the merits which Jesus Christ has secured for the world through His propitiation and vicarious atonement. It is for the infant or the adult, since repentance is given by the grace of God; it matters not the age but both are to be baptized because it works the forgiveness of sins by God's Spirit, who is the gift Peter speaks of.

Peter, in connecting baptism with the forgiveness of sins, is saying nothing else than what the gospel offers and imparts; it works forgiveness of sins, washes away sin, sanctifies and cleanses and regenerates and saves.[57] In the apostle Paul's recounting of his conversion, after he received his sight Ananias says to him, "Rise and be baptized and wash away your sins, calling on His name" (Acts 22:16). Once again we see that the waters of baptism wash away sins because they are connected to the gospel. In Ephesians we read that Christ cleansed "her (the Church) by the washing of water with the word . . ."

56. Mueller, *Christian Dogmatics*, 491.

57. Mueller, *Christian Dogmatics*, 492.

In Paul's letter to the Corinthians, after recalling to them that many were saved out of egregious sins, i.e., sexual immorality, idolaters, adulterers, etc, he does not tell them, "remember you repented of these." Rather, the apostle brings them to Christ and His work in their baptism when he says, "And such were some of you. But you were washed, you were sanctified, you were justified in the name of the Lord Jesus Christ and by the Spirit of our God" (1 Cor 6:11).

If baptism is a simple ceremony at worst and an empty sign and seal at best, which does nothing actually for the sinner, then why is it insisted upon? Why does Paul in Galatians remind believers that at their baptism they actually put on Christ, like clothing (Greek *enduo*) if nothing was actually conferred to them? In Romans 6, Paul writes that those who have been baptized have been buried with Christ and raised with him too. This is not a picture of a reality but the reality itself.

When I went to my pastor in 1986, after my conversion to Christ, I sought to be baptized. I knew this must be done, though I did not know why. I also knew that something happened in baptism and wanted whatever that was. He graciously pointed me to Romans 6 and verses 3–4 stood out to me:

> Do you not know that all of us who have been baptized into Christ Jesus were baptized into his death? We were buried therefore with him by baptism into death, in order that, just as Christ was raised from the dead by the glory of the Father, we too might walk in newness of life.

Here, God's word was saying that in the waters of baptism, with God's word, the old man was being buried by death. That old man was going to die in the waters of baptism and I was going to be raised in newness of life. But hadn't that happened when I repented? Yes and yet baptism was going to bring about all the promises of God, all the blessings He has given His church in those blessed waters. While I did not feel different, in fact, I left the waters thinking something was missing in what I understood about baptism, yet, the reality was that I had died with Christ and was raised with him too in those waters.

As I came to understand the plain reading of the Scriptures, Titus 3:5 began to unravel what had happened:

> *He saved us, not because of works done by us in righteousness, but according to his own mercy, by the washing of regeneration and renewal of the Holy Spirit.*

Since Ephesians states there is one baptism, this "washing of regeneration" connects regeneration to baptism. I wrote earlier that both the Reformed and evangelical view is that there are two baptisms: spiritual and water. Yet Scripture says there is one. Therefore, when one reads about washings or baptism and then of regeneration, in order to remain faithful to God's word, they speak of that one baptism. God works regeneration through baptism and His Word.

Peter actually states that baptism saves. He wrote, "Baptism, which corresponds to (Greek *antitypos*) this, now saves you, not as a removal of dirt from the body but as an appeal to God for a good conscience, through the resurrection of Jesus Christ" (1 Pet 3:21). The early Christians understood that Peter was connecting the waters of baptism with the forgiveness of sins, regeneration, and salvation. Cyprian of Carthage wrote, "Peter showed and vindicated the unity of the church by commanding and warning that we can be saved only through the baptism of the one church . . ."[58]

The writer of Hebrews brings both water and regeneration together when he writes,

> Let us draw near with a true heart in full assurance of faith, with our hearts sprinkled clean from an evil conscience and our bodies washed with pure water. (Heb 10:22)

Why would the writer speak of both our hearts sprinkled and our bodies washed? Is he advocating two baptisms: one spiritual and one by water? Absolutely not! God forbid! That would contradict what Paul, by inspiration of the Holy Spirit, wrote: that there is one baptism. So, the correct conclusion is that when the Scripture

58. Cyprian of Carthage, *Letters* 74.11 (AD 253), quoted in Roseborough, "What the Bible Teaches."

speaks of our hearts being sprinkled it is because in baptism we are cleansed, forgiven, regenerated, buried with Christ and raised with him. New life is in the waters of baptism with the Word.

New Life in the Flood

Martin Luther, in correcting the theology of some ancient prayers, wrote this prayer in his baptismal booklet:

> Almighty and eternal God, according to Your strict judgment You condemned the unbelieving world through the flood, yet according to Your great mercy You preserved believing Noah and his family, eight souls in all. You drowned hard-hearted Pharaoh and all his host in the Red Sea, yet led Your people Israel through the water on dry ground, prefiguring this washing of Your Holy Baptism.
>
> Through the Baptism in the Jordan of Your beloved Son, our Lord Jesus Christ, You sanctified and instituted all waters to be a blessed flood, and a lavish washing away of sin. We pray that You would behold (name) according to Your boundless mercy and bless him with true faith by the Holy Spirit that through this saving flood all sin in him which has been inherited from Adam and which he himself has committed since would be drowned and die. Grant that he be kept safe and secure in the holy ark of the Christian Church, being separated from the multitude of unbelievers and serving Your name at all times with a fervent spirit and a joyful hope, so that, with all believers in Your promise, he would be declared worthy of eternal life, through Jesus Christ, our Lord.[59]

In Noah's flood, sinners were drowned. In the waters of baptism, sin is drowned, both original and sins committed, as well as those of omission. In the flood of the Red Sea, the enemy of God's people, Pharaoh and his army, were drowned. Paul says that the people of God who walked through on dry ground were baptized

59. Mark Birkholz, "Luther's Flood Prayer." https://lutheranreformation.org/history/luthers-flood-prayer/.

into Moses. How much more are we baptized into Christ through the water with the Word.

Next, Luther notes that when Jesus was baptized, He sanctified the baptismal waters and made them a "blessed flood." Through this flood of water new life is given, regeneration happens to the sinner dead in sin and bound to Satan. They are liberated, forgiven, saved because He works through the water and the Word. Finally, just as Noah and his family were saved from the judgment of the flood as they were brought into the ark, so now those who are baptized are baptized into Christ, the true Ark of safety. They are now safe and sound because they have been so united to Christ that His righteousness becomes theirs and the old man has been buried with Christ, having drowned in those blessed flood waters.

When one looks at all the verses of Scripture which speak of the waters of baptism, the being sprinkled clean, the washing of regeneration, and all other references to water, there is an overwhelming argument for the Lutheran, biblical view of baptism. This sacrament truly confers the blessings of the gospel promises in the water and the Word. The water alone does nothing but when joined to the Word of God it is no mere ceremony. Neither is baptism a sign symbolic of a baptism inwardly or a seal in which the letter it signifies has nothing written therein, as Luther complained regarding the Reformed position. Rather, baptism "is, is, is a washing of regeneration" as Dr. Jacob Andreae said in the debate with Dr. Theodore Beza of Geneva.

A Conscience Cleared and Cheered

One of the many issues I struggled with was whether or not I had true faith. In the Reformed catechism (Heidelberg) True faith contains three elements: 1. Knowledge, 2. Assent, and 3. Trust. The Heidelberg puts it this way:

> 21. What is true faith?
>
> True faith is not only a sure knowledge whereby I hold for truth all that God has revealed to us in His Word; but also a hearty trust, which the Holy Spirit

> works in me by the Gospel, that not only to others, but to me also, forgiveness of sins, everlasting righteousness and salvation are freely given by God, merely of grace, only for the sake of Christ's merits.[60]

You actually have to read Question and Answer 20 to understand what is being discussed. The question is whether all men are saved by Christ just as they all perished in Adam. The Answer is: No; but only those who by a true faith are engrafted into Him and receive all His benefits. The catechism then goes on to teach what true faith is. This true faith must have knowledge. Of this, all Christians would agree that one must first know about Jesus, about his life, death, and resurrection, in order to know why they even need a Savior. However, even the Devil and his minions know about Jesus, so knowledge isn't enough. Second, one must assent to these facts as true. Third, one must have a firm confidence that what is spoken of about Jesus is true. This trust is attributed to the work of the Spirit through the proclamation of the gospel. This is where, for me and many Christian women whom I've worked with over the past dozen or so years, have struggled.

First, how do we know we believe all that the Bible says about Jesus? Are there areas where we might have doubt? If we doubt, then it is no longer a "sure knowledge" but an unsure, uncertain knowing. Does this mean I no longer have "true faith"? This, then, effects assent. How can I agree with it if I have doubts? How can those who doubt have their conscience cheered? The catechism taught that it is necessary for a Christian to believe "all that is promised us in the gospel . . ." Again, what if someone has doubts?

Furthermore, if there are doubts then you cannot possibly have a "firm confidence" for they are diametrically opposed to each other. Dr. Andreae argued that one could not be given assurance if they are left to the internal moving of the Spirit, which Calvin said happens for those amongst the elect, since the person already doubts and does not feel the movement of the Spirit. This leads further to deeper doubt and "desperation will increase, not diminish." Unless there is somewhere the struggling, doubting, fearful believer can look, they will be crushed under the weight

60. Ursinus, *Commentary on the Heidelberg Catechism*, loc. 8249, Kindle.

of despair. This was where I landed in my struggles; Am I a true believer?

The biblical understanding is that at baptism all the gospel promises of Christ are given freely to the recipient. It does not matter how "assured" they are in themselves because feelings ebb and flow throughout one's life. However, because baptism is a washing of regeneration and renewal in the Holy Spirit as well as the seal of actually being adopted, one can look to their baptism and say I *am* baptized. The hymn I opened this chapter quoting, "God's Own Child," says it beautifully and warrants quoting it again:

> Sin, disturb my soul no longer:
> *I am baptized into Christ*!
> I have comfort even stronger:
> Jesus' cleansing sacrifice.
> Should a guilty conscience seize me,
> since my baptism did release me
> In a dear forgiving flood,
> sprinkling me with Jesus' blood?
>
> Satan, hear this proclamation:
> *I am baptized into Christ*!
> Drop your ugly accusation;
> I am not so soon enticed.
> Now that to the font I've traveled,
> all your might has come unraveled,
> And, against your tyranny,
> God, my Lord, unites with me!

When I struggled with seeing failing, faulty, and unripe fruit in my life, when the sin that so easily besets would rear its ugly head, or when doubt arose, the words of this hymn would come to mind:

> Sin disturb my soul not longer,
> *I am baptized in Christ*;
> my baptism did release me
> in a dear forgiving flood;

Satan, hear this proclamation,
I am baptized into Christ!
. . . all your might has come unraveled!

Scripture says, against all accusations, "One who believes and is baptized will be saved" (Mark 16:16).

In Luther's Large Catechism he writes on baptism,

> It is of the greatest importance that we value Baptism as excellent, glorious, and exalted. We contend and fight for Baptism chiefly because the world is now so full of sects arguing that Baptism is an outward thing and that outward things are of no benefit. But let Baptism be a thoroughly outward thing. Here stand God's Word and command, which institute, establish, and confirm Baptism. What God institutes and commands cannot be an empty thing. It must be a most precious thing, even though it looked like it had less value than a straw . . . We ought to value Baptism much more highly and more precious, because God has commanded it.[61]

When my heart condemns me, or Satan accuses me, this is the true consolation:

I am baptized into Christ!

61. Dau, *Concordia*, 424.

CHAPTER 5

Comfort

Simple and True

IN MY CHRISTIAN LIFE over the past two and a half decades, the study of God's Word has become preeminent. The changes to my theology, as you have read in this book, have come about because of God's Word. Discussing these changes with my husband along with his encouragement to write this book, he has confirmed over and over to me that the reason we are now Lutheran is because there is complete safety and comfort knowing that what God's word says is what God means. One of the main reasons for this comfort is that God's word actually means what He has said. There is no trying to figure God out, trying to peer into the hidden things of God, the secrets of God, as the Gnostics, Charismatics and many Calvinists attempt to do as opposed to Lutheran interpretation of the Scriptures. Instead, Lutherans receive the Word of God and understand that, as my friend Sally reminds me, "God is a lot smarter than we are." As Lutherans we live with the tensions that are in the Holy Scriptures and believe that God knows what He is doing and it will all work out in the end. We do not try to go beyond what Scripture plainly teaches but simply receive it as He has spoken it through His written word. In this, there is so much comfort because I no longer have to figure out God. His word tells me plainly what I need to know for salvation and assurance.

In the formula of Concord Article 7, "On the Holy Supper of Christ," it states, "We believe, teach, and confess that the words of Christ's testament are not to be understood in any other way then the way they read, according to the letter."[1] Lutherans hold firmly to what the Scriptures teach without addendums or explanations that refer to some hidden meaning. No, Lutherans read Scripture as Scripture speaks.

The Lutheran assumptions in biblical interpretation are as follows

> God's word, because it is his word, is without error. That means the Bible cannot lie or deceive and that God's word is the only rule for faith in life.
>
> Christ is the heart and center of God's word. This means the doctrine of justification by God's grace through faith in Christ is the chief doctrine of the Scriptures. Also, Christian should carefully distinguish long gospel.
>
> The Holy Spirit helps us to understand God's word. This means difficult passages of Scripture are to be interpreted by other, clearer passages. Also, as we read scripture, in humility we derive the plain meaning of words from their literal sense, unless clearly directed otherwise by context.[2]

Often, when reading the Scriptures, I can hear in the back of my mind the words of Gandalf: "You shall not pass . . ."[3] The reason that phrase comes back to me over and over is that when I was Reformed I would always be looking for a deeper meaning, rather than simply reading and interpreting the words that were written. However, as a Lutheran I have relearned how to read the Scriptures for what it plainly says. It is rather simple, actually, you read them

1. Dau, *Concordia*, 424.

2. Engelbrecht, *Lutheran Difference*, 4.

3. Peter Jackson, dir. *The Lord of the Rings: The Fellowship of the Ring*. 2001, Burbank, CA: New Line Cinema.

so the words that they say, "unless clearly directed otherwise by contexts"[4] mean what they say.

I remember explaining it to the ladies in the Tuesday Bible study at church that it often felt like I was doing some theological gymnastics when interpreting God's word. Instead of just accepting what his Word said, even if I didn't comprehend it all, I would be trying to jump through hoops weren't even there. When reading the passage in Peter on baptism where he says "baptism now saves you" (1 Pet 3:19–21) I would try to explain that away as a spiritual baptism. However, that is not what the Bible says. Peter is talking about *water* baptism. He uses the flood account of Noah, which is water, and correlates that to the floodwaters of baptism and says "baptism now saves you" (1 Pet 3:19). So in my Reformed mind I would try to take this square peg with clear-cut delineations and shove it into a round hole that was my Reformed interpretation box. It never did fit. In the same way my heart longed for more in the Lord's Supper because I was taught this was only a spiritual food symbolized in the elements of bread and wine, I would try to fit this square peg in the round hole as well.

Over and over in this book I have shared the struggles I had, the doubts and the interpretation difficulties that I went through when I was a Dutch Reformed Calvinist. I did not become Lutheran intentionally but accidently due to Snowmageddon which God used to bring us to Faith Lutheran. However, as my pastor wrote in the foreword, I soon became intentionally Lutheran as I read every book and article he passed along to me, comparing it with the Bible. Although for certain many of our Presbyterian and Reformed friends often said to us, "You two are more Lutheran than reformed . . ." sometimes it takes me a little bit to get it, but I got it. I am not Lutheran for any other reason than simply because these truths align best with what the word of God plainly says. I am not Lutheran because Martin Luther and all the princes and elders and electors realized that these were the biblical truths, but because what they recovered *is* what the word of God simply teaches us.

4. Engelbrecht, *Lutheran Difference*, 4.

In writing this book I wanted to explain to my many friends who are Baptist, Pentecostal, Presbyterian and various types of Reformed Christians, why both my husband and I converted to Lutheranism. It was not intentional but quite *Providential*. My dissertation for my doctorate was on the Providence of God. Through that study the emphasis on God's directing His creation, His children, and His church became clearer and clearer to me. When Bobby was diagnosed with prostate cancer the comfort I had was that God was in total control even though my world felt exactly the opposite. This understanding of God's Sovereignty is what made the transition from Dutch Reformed or Heidelberg to Lutheranism or Wittenberg so much easier. These truths align with God's word without jumping through hoops or theological contortions.

You see that God directs all things and that the weather is most certainly in His hands; the rough winter which hindered us from attending church in Boise, aka Snowmageddon and the longing to partake of the Lord's Supper because I was beginning to understand that we are fed by Him and our faith is strengthened through Him, all led to us looking at Faith Lutheran Church here in town. Knowing that when God's children are looking for something more biblical is primarily because God is putting that desire in their heart made the transition quicker and easier.

The Warnings are Real

There were other teachings which I struggled with as a Dutch Reformed Gal (as I was often called) which I could not rectify with the Scriptures. One of the major issues was when we were in Canada at the 500th Anniversary Celebration of the Heidelberg Confession, several members would introduce us as new Christians because we had only recently become Reformed. That always bothered me. When I questioned their reason for saying we were not Christians until we became Reformed, their response was that until one came to a Reformed understanding of Scripture, one was not truly saved. In my logically thinking brain I had to imagine God's church without true believers from about the eighth century until the fifteenth when the recovery of the true gospel happened under Martin Luther. Then I began to think, well, if Luther did not come to a "Reformed" understanding, were they saying he too was lost? This bothered me.

Another key teaching was that of the warning passages in the Scriptures. We are told in Hebrews that some had "tasted" but had walked away, going back to the temple sacrificial system. In other places Christians are encouraged to persevere until the end in order to receive the crown of life. If these were empty threats that believers could walk away from Jesus Christ and Him crucified, then was God telling a lie? My thinking goes like this:

God makes the threat but knows He will never carry it out. This means believers can behave badly because the threat of losing salvation isn't really true. If God knows the threats against falling away are not true, then He would be pushing a falsehood . . . and we know God does not lie. Therefore, those threats must be real, the warnings are true, and we must trust His grace to keep us.

Absolution

Here is a teaching which the Lutheran church has held since Christ gave the keys of the Kingdom to the disciples. Here, at the beginning of the divine service after confession, the pastor tells us that as he stands there in the stead of Christ, our sins are forgiven. Talking to my dear friend Lee Ann, we would regale how our jaws dropped to the floor the first time we heard this. What, our mind would say, that's a man telling us we're forgiven? How can he do that? Well, as we both came to understand Scripture more, we understood that this is one of the gifts Christ gave to the church; the pastor is able to tell us our sins are forgiven and we are right with God.

I have not focused upon the warnings and absolution much in this book because the two main teachings of the Bible which Lutherans have rightly maintained, are baptism, which now saves, and the Lord's Supper, His true body and blood given for the forgiveness of our sins; these were the catalysts God used to bring us to Wittenberg. These past years I have found the warnings to be more sobering and absolution to be more comforting. However, let me share some lessons I have learned about confession and absolution as this is where comfort and joy are to be found.

In the Lutheran Divine Services, there are several forms of this prayer of confession which we make, together as a congregation, each Sunday:

> *Pastor: Let us then confess our sins to God our Father,*
>
> *Congregation: Most merciful God, we confess that we are by nature sinful and unclean. We have sinned against You in thought, word, and deed, by what we have done and by what we have left undone. We have not loved You with our whole heart; we have no loved our neighbors as ourselves. We justly deserve Your present and eternal punishment. For the sake of Your Son, Jesus Christ, have mercy on us. Forgive us, renew us, and lead us, so that we may delight in Your will and walk in Your ways to the glory of Your holy name. Amen.*
>
> *Pastor: Almighty God in His mercy has given His Son to die for you and for His sake forgives you all your sins. As a called and ordained servant of Christ, and by His authority, I therefore forgive you all your sins in the name of the Father and of the Son and of the Holy Spirit (John 20:19–23).*[5]

This last part is called absolution. Our sins forgiven as the pastor, a called and ordained servant by God's authority forgives us our sins in the Triune Name. Absolution was one area that shocked me when first becoming Lutheran. However, there are two places in Scripture where Christ Jesus gives His disciples the authority to forgive sins: Matthew 16:19 and John 20:19–23. In both of these places Christ gives them authority to both withhold forgiveness for those unrepentant—an example of which is Paul's use of the keys for the impenitent man having sex with his stepmother (1 Cor 5:13)—and opening up heaven with forgiveness through the proclamation of the gospel and declaring absolution for believers who struggle with sin daily.

5. Lutheran Church Missouri Synod, *Lutheran Service Book*, 167, Divine Service Two.

Ah, comfort. I cannot tell you how it feels to hear in your own ears that you are absolved of your sins. It was indeed strange at the beginning but now each week I look forward to hearing it said to me and the congregation, that our sins are forgiven and heaven's doors are open. Now I know both my evangelical and reformed friends will remind me that I can repent any time, any day for any and every sin. Oh, that is so true and yet, there is great comfort in hearing, from the man, whom God has called and ordained, that your sins are forgiven in the Triune Name.

Complete Safety

After my dissertation was published I then broke it down to a year-long devotional titled: "A Mighty Comfort." The problem with this was that in my dissertation I made God the author of sin, that He planned the Fall and that those who are elect are secure no matter what. From this I have often felt guilty for teaching it and have confessed the sin of this horrific teaching. However, when struggling with whether or not one is of the elect of God, one cannot ever be sure because that faith which they have, as Calvin put it, may not be a true faith even though it looks real, sounds real, and lives out in the world like real faith. The unbeliever may simply have false faith but they would never know it because it has all the fruits of true faith and yet simply isn't true faith. That, my friend, is not comfort but confusion. That, my friend, is an unsafe life with many rabbit holes of doubt one can get stuck in.

Yet, there is complete safety and comfort knowing that what God's word says is what He means and that He means exactly what He says. Amongst the various styles and versions of Christianity which I've traveled, be they Pentecostal, Charismatic, Reformed Baptist, or Dutch Reformed, I have not found this solid ground upon which I can safely stand except in Lutheranism. Lutherans are Lutheran; we are biblical and simply say that what God's word says we believe, or as the catechism says, "This is most certainly true." As Lutherans, we take comfort that God's word and the message of His grace is simple and true.

Please do not think that I do not consider my friends in other theological groups to not belong to Jesus Christ. His church is, indeed, worldwide and His grace is effective in the lives of those who place their trust in His good works and not theirs to either become a Christian or stay one. There are many in the Reformed camp that I respect and still refer to. The gospel is simple and His grace remains true that He will build His church and the gates of hell will not prevail against her. I love my Baptist and Reformed brothers and sisters and pray that one day they will journey from where they are now, through God's providential leadings, all the way to the church of the Augsburg Confession at Wittenberg.

I may have titled this book *The* Accidental *Lutheran* but by no means do I think God did not providentially lead my husband Bobby and I to Lutheranism. It is exactly as my pastor, Rev. Kellerman wrote: I am now a very intentional Lutheran. Therefore, with the same conviction which Martin Luther had at the Diet of Worms, I too am convinced of these interpretations of Scripture and I echo his words when I write:

Unless I am convinced by the testimony
of the Scriptures and by clear reason,
I am bound by the Scriptures I have quoted.
My conscience is captive to the Word of God.
I cannot and will not recant anything
for to go against conscience is neither right nor safe.
Here I stand. I can do no other so help me God. Amen.

—MARTIN LUTHER, DIET OF WORMS

Bibliography

Almodovar, Nancy. *Faith Seeking Unspeakable Consolation*. Eugene, OR: Wipf & Stock, 2013.

Andreae, Jakob, and Clinton J. Armstrong. *Lutheranism Vs. Calvinism: The Classic Debate at the Colloquy of Montbâeliard 1586*. St. Louis: Concordia, 2017.

Baptist Distinctives. "Baptists' Two Ordinances: Baptism and the Lord's Supper." https://www.baptistdistinctives.org/resources/articles/two-ordinances-baptism-and-the-lords-supper/.

Beveridge, Henry, ed. and trans. "Mutual Consent of the Churches of Zurich and Geneva as to the Sacraments." In *Treatises on the Sacraments*. Fearn, Ross-shire: Christian Heritage, 2002. Quoted at: https://calvinistinternational.com/2013/03/14/the-sacraments-do-not-confer-grace/.

Bickle, David R. "Seeing the Forgiveness of God: The sacraments from John Calvin's perspective." http://dawningrealm.org/sacraments/calvin/.

Calvin, John. *Calvin: Institutes of the Christian Religion*. The Library of Christian Classics 21. Presbyterian Publishing Corporation. Kindle Edition.

Chemnitz, Martin. *Chemnitz's Works*. Vol. 5. St. Louis: Concordia, 2007.

Chrysostom. "Homily 60 on Matthew." New Advent. http://www.newadvent.org/fathers/200160.htm.

Cooper, Jordan. *The Great Divide*. Eugene, OR: Wipf & Stock, 2015.

Dau, William Hermann Theodore. *Concordia: The Lutheran Confessions : A Reader's Edition of the Book of Concord*, 425–26. St. Louis: Concordia, 2005.

Ecumenical and Reformed Creeds and Confessions. Classroom Edition. Hospers, IA: Mid-America Reformed Seminary, 1991.

Engelbrecht, Edward A. *The Lutheran Difference: An Explanation & Comparison of Christian Beliefs*. St. Louis: Concordia, 2010.

"Four Views of the Lord's Supper." http://www.twoagespilgrims.com/pasigucrc/2012/05/03/four-views-of-the-lords-supper/.

Heschmeyer, Joe. "Evanescent Grace." http://shamelesspopery.com/assurance-of-salvation-and-evanescent-grace/.

Lehmann, Charles R. *Lutheranism 101: Holy Baptism*. St. Louis: Concordia, 2013.

London Baptist Confession of Faith. "Chapter 30: Of the Lord's Supper." 1689. http://www.vor.org/truth/1689/1689bc30.html.

Luther, Martin. *Luther's Small Catechism, with Explanation*. St. Louis: Concordia, 2017.

Lutheran Church Missouri Synod. *Lutheran Service Book: Three-year Lectionary*. St. Louis: Concordia, 2006.

Kampen, Eric. "The Means of Grace." *Clarion Magazine* 60.23 546.

Merriam Webster Dictionary. "Ordinance." https://www.merriam-webster.com/dictionary/ordinance.

Mueller, John Theodore. *Christian Dogmatics: A Handbook of Doctrinal Theology for Pastors, Teachers, and Laymen*, 492–93. St. Louis: Concordia, 1934.

Plass, Ewald M. *What Luther Says, an Anthology*. St. Louis: Concordia, 1959.

Rosebrough, Chris. "What the Bible Teaches About Baptism & How the Earliest Christians Understood These Biblical Texts." http://0352182.netsolhost.com/Baptism%20Texts%20%26%20the%20Earliest%20Christians.pdf.

Sasse, Herman. *This Is My Body: Luther's Contention for the Real Presence in the Sacrament of the Altar*. Minneapolis: Augsburg, 1959.

Schwertley, Brian. *The Sacraments, A Reformed Perspective*. http://www.reformedonline.com/uploads/1/5/0/3/15030584/the_sacraments_a_reformed_perspective.pdf.

Sproul, R.C. "The Focus of Sacraments." Ligonier Ministries. https://www.ligonier.org/learn/devotionals/the-focus-of-the-sacraments/.

Ursinus, Zacharias. *Commentary on the Heidelberg Catechism*. Grand Rapids: Eerdmans, 1954.

Veith, Gene Edward, Jr. *The Spirituality of the Cross: The Way of the First Evangelicals*. St. Louis: Concordia, 1999.

Wieting, Kenneth. *Lutheranism 101: The Lord's Supper*. St. Louis: Concordia, 2015.

www.ingramcontent.com/pod-product-compliance
Lightning Source LLC
Chambersburg PA
CBHW071057090426
42737CB00013B/2359